서울미식
안내서

100 TASTE OF SEOUL 2022

100 Restaurants & Bars in Seoul
KOREAN · ENGLISH

미식도시 서울,
세계로 나아갑니다.

오랜 궁궐과 고층 빌딩이 한곳에 모여 있듯 전통과 현대가
공존하고 자연과 첨단이 어우러진 서울은 고유한 미식
문화로도 세계의 주목을 받고 있습니다.

서울시는 서울만의 다양하고 차별화된 미식문화를
국내외로 알리기 위해 20 미식 큐레이터 및 전문가와 함께
'서울 레스토랑&바 100선'을 선정하는
'테이스트오브서울 100선' 프로젝트를 올해로 3회째 진행
했습니다. 한식뿐만 아니라 양식, 아시안, 그릴과 채식,
카페&디저트, 바&펍에 이르기까지, 분야별로
'글로컬리즘', '전문성', '이슈성' 등을 고려해 서울미식을
대표할 만한 100곳을 담았습니다.

어려운 시기에도 최고의 미식 경험을 선사하기 위해
최선을 다하고 계시는 모든 외식업계 분들께 감사와
응원을 드리며, 서울이 '미식'이라는 언어로 세계로
뻗어가며 함께 성장하기를 바랍니다.

앞으로도 매년 정기적인 발굴과 조사를 통해 의미 있는
'서울미식 안내서'로 성장해가겠습니다.

Seoul: a city of taste, advancing into the world

Seoul, a city of historical palaces surrounded by skyscrapers where tradition meets modernity and nature harmonizes with advanced technology, is drawing the world's attention with its unique gourmet culture.

To promote the diverse and differentiated gourmet culture of Seoul, Seoul Metropolitan Government (SMG) has implemented the "Taste of Seoul - Seoul Restaurants & Bars 100" project this year as the third iteration to select the city's top 100 restaurants and bars together with 20 gourmet curators and experts. Representing the Taste of Seoul, Seoul Restaurants & Bars 100 were selected by category ranging from Korean, Western, and Asian to Grill, Plant-based, Café & Dessert, and Bar & Pub with consideration given to the elements of "glocalism," "expertise," and "public interest."

We would like to express our gratitude and appreciation to the people in the food service industry who are doing their best to present the best gourmet experiences despite the difficulties of the times. We hope that Seoul will advance into the world with the language of "gourmet."

We will continue developing Taste of Seoul - Seoul Restaurants & Bars 100 as a reliable guidebook for the tastes that Seoul has to offer by discovering new restaurants and bars based on surveys conducted each year.

업장 정보 아이콘
Information Icon

배달 가능 메뉴 있음
Delivery menus available

테이크아웃 가능 메뉴 있음
Take-out menus available

주차 가능(발렛 포함)
Parking (including valet parking service) available

별실 있음
Private room available

테라스 있음
Terrace available

비건 메뉴 있음   100% 비건 메뉴
Vegan menus available   **100% Vegan menus available**

CONTENTS

한식
Korean ——— 23

아시안
Asian ——— 51

양식
Western ——— 63

그릴
Grill ——— 93

채식
Plant-based ——— 103

카페 & 디저트
Café & Dessert ——— 115

바 & 펍
Bar & Pub ——— 129

채식 맛집 50선
50 Plant-based ——— 144

인덱스
Index ——— 198

*음식 이미지는 실제와 다를 수 있습니다.
*The food in the picture may look different from the actual food.

*영업시간은 코로나19 상황에 따라 달라질 수 있습니다.
*Business hours may vary depending on the COVID-19 social distancing regulations.

한눈에 보는 2022 테이스트오브서울 100선

미식 큐레이터 서베이를 통해 집계된, 서울에서 꼭 방문해야 할 레스토랑과 바 100곳에 대한 결과를 한눈에 살펴본다.

숫자로 보는 서베이

20
미식 큐레이터

85 15
내국인 외국인

7
카테고리

21
큐레이터당 레스토랑 & 바 추천 수

◆ 큐레이터 구성 ◆

50%
업계 전문가

15%
미식 여행가

15%
학자

20%
식음 저널리스트

추천 원칙

지난 2년간 방문한 곳 중 '글로컬리즘', '전문성', '화제성'을 고려하여 최고라고 생각하는 곳을 장르별로 3곳씩 순서대로 기입.

우선 추천한 곳일수록 높은 점수 부여.

레스토랑은 반드시 '셰프'가 있는 곳으로, 바는 반드시 '바텐더(또는 이에 준하는 역할)'가 있는 곳을 추천한다.

본인이 근무하거나 이해관계가 있는 곳은 제외된다.

Taste of Seoul

퀴진별 세부 비율

전체 100곳 중 29곳이 지난해(2021년)와 다른 신규 업장으로 선정됐다. 퀴진으로 분류하면, 한식 23곳, 아시안 10곳, 양식 26곳, 그릴 8곳, 채식 9곳, 카페 & 디저트 11곳, 바 & 펍 13곳으로 구성됐다.

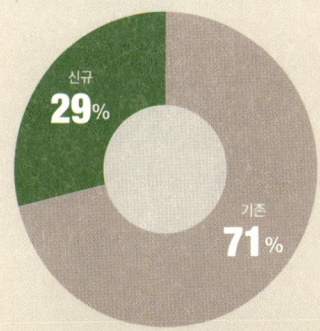
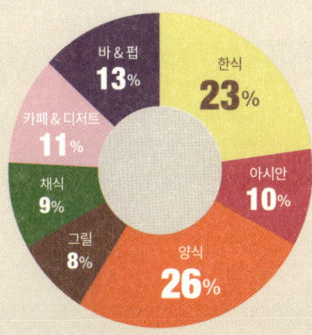

한식

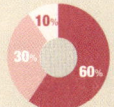

한식은 전통과 모던 사이에서 다채로운 변주를 보여주는 장르다. 총 23곳은 한식 30.5%(7곳), 모던 한식 39%(9곳), 전통 한식 30.5%(7곳)으로 나타났다.

- 한식
- 모던 한식
- 전통 한식

아시안

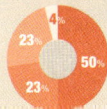

아시안 업장 10곳 중 중식이 60%(6곳)로 가장 높은 비중을 차지했다. 그 뒤를 이어 일식 30%(3곳), 타이 10%(1곳) 순으로 다양성을 보였다.

- 중식
- 일식
- 타이

양식

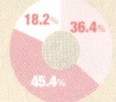

양식 업장 26곳 중에서 프렌치가 50%(13곳)로 절반을 차지했다. 이탤리언과 이노베이티브가 각각 23%(6곳)로 같은 비율을 보였고, 나머지 4%(1곳)는 지중해식이었다.

- 프렌치
- 이탤리언
- 이노베이티브
- 지중해식

카페 & 디저트

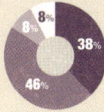

카페 & 디저트 업장 11곳은 서양 디저트 45.4%(5곳), 한식 디저트 36.4%(4곳), 베이커리와 카페 18.2%(2곳) 순으로 나타났다.

- 서양 디저트
- 한식 디저트
- 베이커리 & 카페

바 & 펍

바 & 펍 업장 13곳 중에서 칵테일 바가 46%(6곳)로 제일 높은 비중을 보였고, 와인 바가 38%(5곳)로 그 뒤를 이었다. 전통 주점과 브루어리 & 펍은 각각 8%(1곳)씩 차지했다.

- 와인 바
- 칵테일 바
- 전통 주점
- 브루어리 & 펍

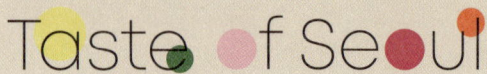

서울 구별 지역 분포

100곳의 업장 중 제일 많은 34곳이 '강남구'에 위치해 지난해에 이어 올해도 여전한 강세를 유지했다. 코로나19 이후 소비 패턴이 고급화하면서 압구정, 청담 쪽의 파인 다이닝 업장들로 발길이 몰리고 있다는 분석이 나온다. 그 뒤를 잇는 지역은 19곳이 분포된 '용산구'다. 거리두기 해제 이후 이태원과 한남동 일대가 활성화되고, 신용산역 인근 용리단길이 특히 MZ세대의 '핫플'로 떠오른 영향으로 보인다. 이외에도 4대궁이 위치해 전통과 현대의 조화를 이루는 '종로구'에 16곳, 뉴트로 열풍의 중심지인 을지로가 있는 '중구'에 10곳이 분포됐다.

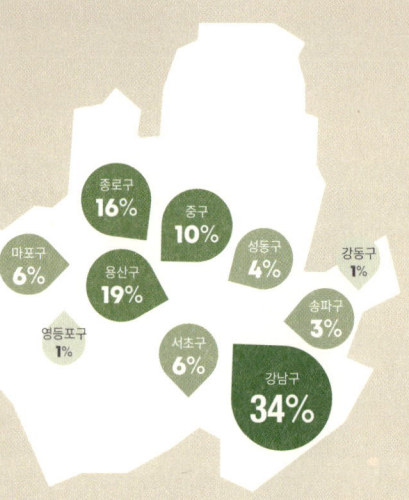

비건 옵션의 강세

전체 100곳 중 비건 옵션 메뉴가 있는 업장은 절반에 가까운 49%로 드러났다. 지난해 48%보다 1%p 증가한 수치다. 지속가능성의 기치 아래 세계적으로 부는 '식물성 열풍'이 서울에도 번지고 있다는 점을 보여준다. 이런 트렌드에 따라, 서울시는 올해 새롭게 '채식 맛집 50선'을 추가로 선정했다.

서울미식에 대한 키워드

패널들에게 '서울미식'에 대한 생각을 물었을 때, 다음과 같은 키워드가 강조되었다.

Taste of Seoul 2022 at a Glance

Here are the results of the survey on the 100 must-visit restaurants and bars in Seoul as recommended by gourmet curators.

Survey Results in Numbers

20
Gourmet Curators

85 15
Locals Foreigners

7
Categories

21
Restaurants and Bars Recommended by Each Curator

♦ **Composition of Curators** ♦

50%
Industry Experts

15%
Gourmet Travelers

15%
Academicians

20%
Food Journalists

Principles of Recommendation

By category, select the three best restaurants and bars visited by the curator for the past two years in terms of "glocalism," "expertise," and "public interest" factors.

Give higher points according to the priority of recommendation.

The recommended restaurants must have a "chef," and bars must have a "bartender (or a person playing an equivalent role)."

Exclude restaurants and bars where the curator works or has personal interest.

Taste of Seoul

Detailed Ratios by Cuisine

29 out of 100 restaurants and bars were selected as new businesses different from those of last year (2021). The 100 restaurants and bars selected are categorized into Korean cuisine (23), Asian cuisine (10), Western cuisine (26), Grill (8), Plant-based (9), Café & Dessert (11), and Bar & Pub (13).

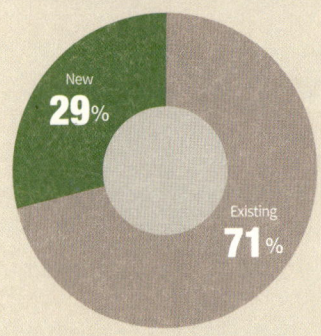
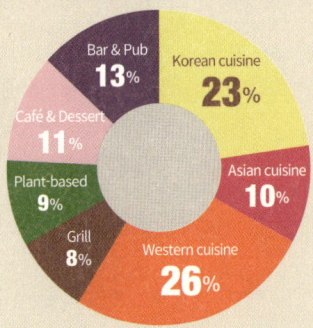

Korean cuisine

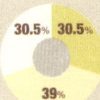

Korean cuisine is a genre that offers interesting variations between traditional and modern styles. The 23 restaurants selected were divided into Korean restaurants (30.5% or 7), modern Korean restaurants (39% or 9), and traditional Korean restaurants (30.5% or 7).

■ Korean ■ Modern Korean ■ Traditional Korean

Asian cuisine

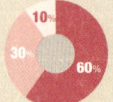

Among the 10 Asian restaurants selected, Chinese restaurants accounted for the largest percentage with 60% (6 restaurants). It was followed by Japanese with 30% (3) and Thai with 10% (1), displaying diversity.

■ Chinese ■ Japanese ■ Thai

Western cuisine

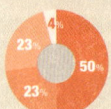

Half (50%) of the 26 Western restaurants selected were French restaurants (13). Next were Italian and Innovative with 23% (6 restaurants each), followed by Mediterranean with 4% (1).

■ French ■ Italian ■ Innovative ■ Mediterranean

Café & Dessert

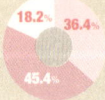

Among the 11 Café & Dessert restaurants selected, Western dessert restaurants accounted for 45.4% (5), followed by Korean dessert with 36.4% (4) and bakery and café with 18.2% (2).

■ Dessert ■ Korean Dessert ■ Bakery & Café

Bar & Pub

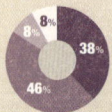

Among the 13 Bar & Pub establishments, cocktail bars constituted the largest percentage with 46% (6) followed by wine bars with 38% (5). Next came traditional liquor bars and breweries & pubs with 8% (1 each).

■ Wine Bar ■ Cocktail Bar ■ Traditional Liquor Bar ■ Brewery & Pub

Taste of Seoul

Distribution by District in Seoul

34 out of the 100 restaurants and bars selected are located in Gangnam-gu, displaying the highest concentration again following last year. This is because the consumption pattern has evolved toward pursuing premium quality since the outbreak of COVID-19, and consumers are naturally drawn to fine dining restaurants in Apgujeong-dong and Cheongdam-dong. 19 restaurants and bars, the second largest number, are located in Yongsan-gu. The lifting of social distancing regulations revitalized the areas around Itaewon and Hannam-dong. In particular, Yongnidan-gil near Sinyongsan Station has emerged as a "hot place" among the Generation MZ. In addition, 16 restaurants and bars are in Jongno-gu, an area with the Four Palaces of Seoul where tradition meets modernity; ten are in Jung-gu where Eulji-ro, the center of the newtro culture, is located.

- Jongno-gu **16%**
- Jung-gu **10%**
- Mapo-gu **6%**
- Yongsan-gu **19%**
- Seongdong-gu **4%**
- Gangdong-gu **1%**
- Yeongdeungpo-gu **1%**
- Seocho-gu **6%**
- Songpa-gu **3%**
- Gangnam-gu **34%**

Vegan Options Emerging as a Hot Trend

49% or almost half of the 100 restaurants and bars offer vegan menu options. This is a 1%p increase from 48% last year. This suggests that the "popularity of plant-based food," which is spreading across the world, for upholding the value of sustainability is also imminent in Seoul. In keeping with this trend, SMG additionally selected the "50 Plant-based Restaurants" this year.

Keywords for Seoul Gourmet Culture

When the panel of curators and experts were asked for their thoughts on "Seoul Gourmet Culture," the following keywords were highlighted:

- FAST DEVELOPMENT
- CREATIVE
- DIVERSITY
- DYNAMIC
- CONVERGENCE OF GENRES
- COEXISTENCE OF TRADITION AND MODERNITY
- FERMENTATION
- GLOBAL
- YOUNG ENERGY

2022 서울술 정복하기

다양한 서울술의 양조장 정보, 주재료, 도수, 맛 속성, 술의 종류 등을 광화문 광장에서 한 눈에!

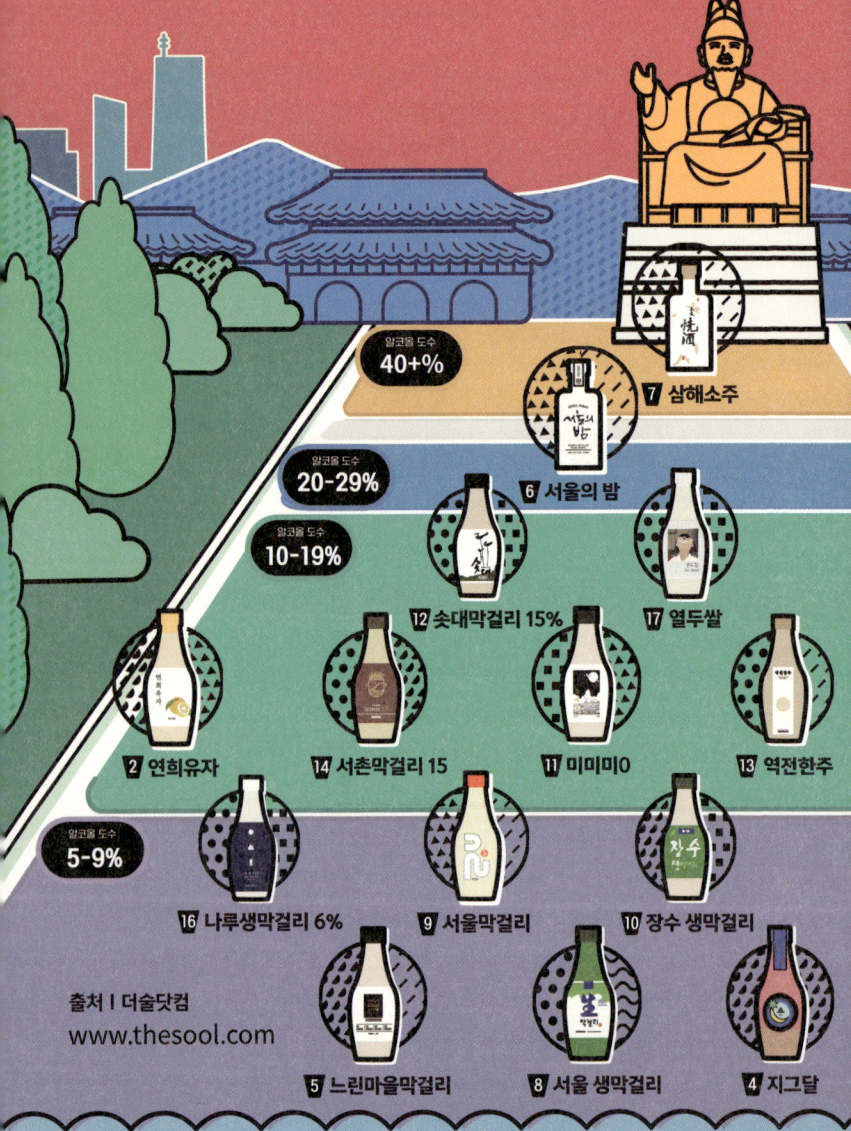

맛 속성 알아보기

서울술의 맛 속성은 크게 6가지로 나누어 표기했습니다.

단맛　　　신맛

향　　　목넘김

바디감　　탄산감

원형 구역 안의 패턴을 통해 각 술의 맛을 파악할 수 있도록 가장 두드러지는 두 가지 특성을 담았습니다.

양조장 알아보기

 제품명 — 제품명 앞의 번호로 서울술이 만들어진 양조장을 알 수 있습니다.

개성 있는 서울술 양조장 **16곳**

※ 🍶 로 표기된 양조장은 음식점을 겸하고 있습니다.

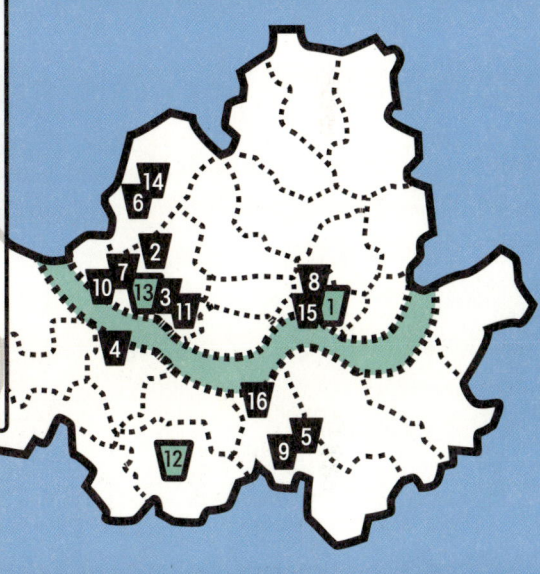

1	**188양조장** · · · · · · · · · · · · · 성동구 성덕정19길 22 2층
2	**같이** · · · · · · · · · · · · · · · · · · 서대문구 증가로 26
3	**구름아양조장** · · · · · · · · 마포구 토정로14길 16 1층 일부
4	**날씨양조** · · · 영등포구 도림로125가길 4-4 골목길 파란대문
5	**느린마을양조장(배상면주가)** 서초구 강남대로27길 7-9외 6곳
6	**더한수류** · · · · · · · · · · · · · · · 은평구 증산로7길 28-13
7	**삼해소주가** · · · · · · · · · 마포구 월드컵북로 109 지하1호
8	**서울생주조** · · · · · 성동구 광나루로8길 19 지산탁주공장
9	**서울양조장** · · · 서초구 효령로34길 7 정서빌딩 4층 402-A호
10	**서울탁주제조협회** · · · · · 마포구 망원로 25 오일빌딩3층
11	**서울효모방** · · 마포구 백범로 13 신촌르메이에르타운Ⅱ 408호
12	**솟대막걸리·양조장** · · · · · · · · · 관악구 신림로 305 3층
13	**역전회관** · · · · · · · · · · · · · · · 마포구 토정로 37길 47
14	**온지술도가** · · · · · · · · · · · · · · · 은평구 통일로 65길 26
15	**한강주조** · · · · · · · · · · · · · · · 성동구 둘레15길 12 2층
16	**한아양조** · · · · · · · · · · · · 서초구 동광로1길 95 101호

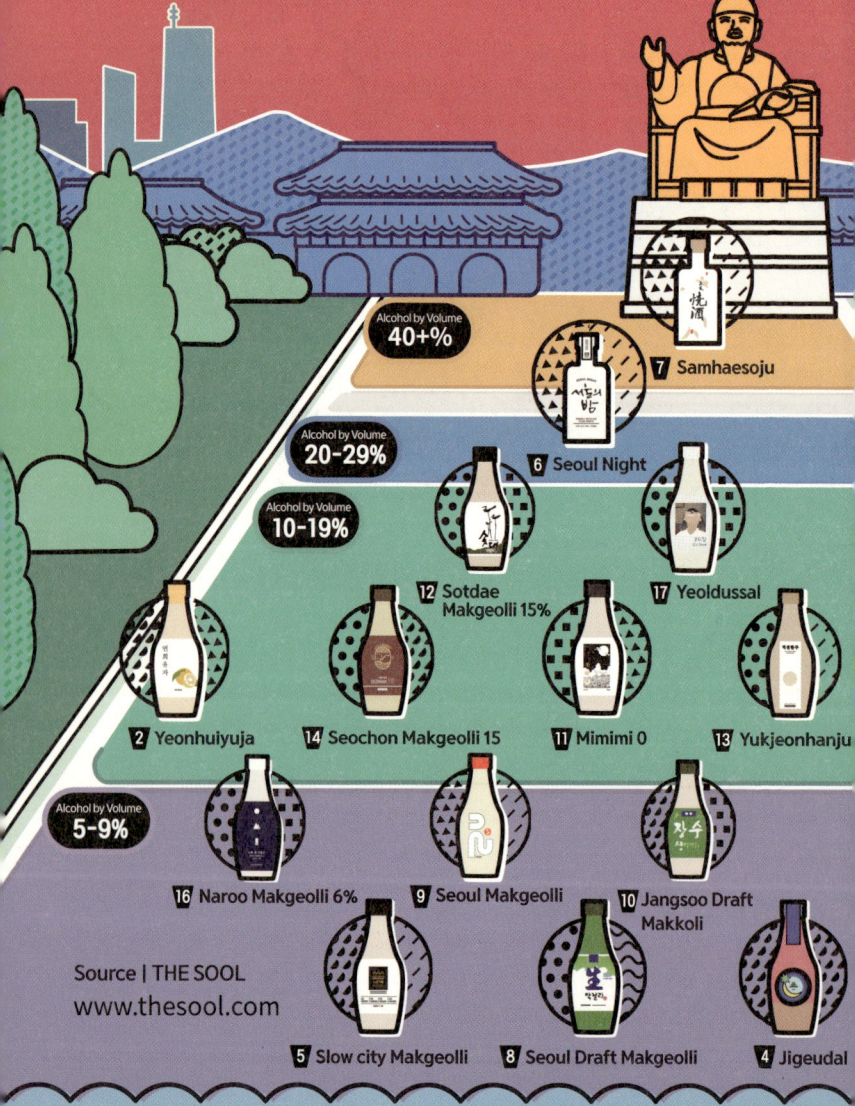

Taste Attributes

The taste attributes of Seoul Liquors are largely divided into the following:

Sweetness

Acidity

Aroma

Texture

Body

Carbonation

The two most distinct attributes of each liquor are displayed with different patterns in a circle.

Breweries in Seoul

 Find the breweries for Seoul Liquors by using the numbers displayed in front of each product name.

16 Seoul Liquor Breweries

※ Breweries marked with also operate restaurants.

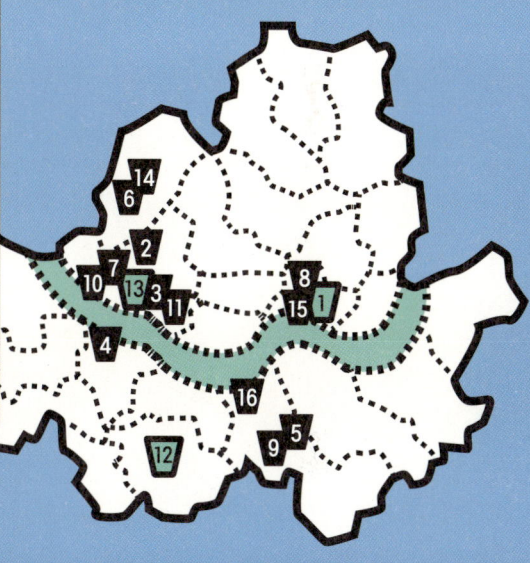

3 Daegwallamcha

13 Yukjeonju

1 Doggaebibul

1	**188 Brewery**	2F, 22, Seongdeokjeong 19-gil, Seongdong-gu
2	**Together Brewery**	26, Jeungga-ro, Seodaemun-gu
3	**Guruma Brewery**	1F, 16, Tojeong-ro 14-gil, Mapo-gu
4	**Weather Brewery**	Blue Gate on Alley, 4-4, Dorim-ro 125ga-gil, Yeongdeungpo-gu
5	**Slow City Brewery (Bae&Brewing Co.)**	7-9, Gangnam-daero 27-gil, Seocho-gu and six other locations
6	**The Han Liquor**	28-13, Jeungsan-ro 7-gil, Eunpyeong-gu
7	**Samhaesojuga**	B1, 109, World Cup buk-ro, Mapo-gu
8	**Seoul Saeng Corp.**	Jisantakju Factory, 19, Gwangnaru-ro 8-gil, Seongdong-gu
9	**Seoul Brewery**	402-A, 4F, Jeongseo Building, 7, Hyoryeong-ro 34-gil, Seocho-gu
10	**Seoul Takju Manufacturers Association**	3F, Oil Building, 25, Mangwon-ro, Mapo-gu
11	**Seoul fermentary**	408, Sinchon Le Meilleur Town II, 13, Baekbeom-ro, Mapo-gu
12	**Sotdae Makgeolli & Brewery**	3F, 305, Sillim-ro, Gwanak-gu
13	**Yukjeonhoegwan**	47, Tojeong-ro 37-gil, Mapo-gu
14	**Onzi Brewery**	26, Tongil-ro 65-gil, Eunpyeong-gu
15	**Hangang Brewery**	2F, 12, Dulle 15-gil, Seongdong-gu
16	**Hanayangjo**	101, 95, Donggwang-ro 1-gil, Seocho-gu

Korean

한식

가온
Gaon

권숙수
Kwonsooksoo

꽃, 밥에 피다
A Flower Blossom on the Rice

남도제철맛집
Nam Do Jecheol

라연
La Yeon

레스토랑 주은
Restaurant Jueun

마포옥
Mapo-ok

무궁화
Mugunghwa

밍글스
Mingles

봉피양 방이점
Bon Pi Yang

비채나
Bicena

세븐스도어
7th Door

소설 한남
SOSEOUL hannam

스와니예
SOIGNÉ

안씨 막걸리
Mr. Ahn's Craft Makgeolli

온지음 레스토랑
ONJIUM

용수산 비원
Yong Su San

우래옥
Woo Lae Oak

윤서울
YUN SEOUL

을밀대
Eul Mil Dae

이타닉 가든
Eatanic Garden

정식당
JUNGSIKDANG

주옥
Joo Ok

가온 한식 Korean
Gaon

프리미엄 도자 브랜드 광주요의 한식 다이닝이다. 한식에 대한 깊은 연구로 식재료 본연의 맛을 풍부하게 끌어올리는 김병진 셰프의 요리가 멋스러운 식기와 어우러진다. 10년 숙성 씨간장 양념에 부드럽게 쪄낸 전복찜은 특히 호평을 받는 메뉴.

Gaon is a Korean restaurant by premium china brand KwangJuYo. Fine china dinnerware harmonizes well with the dishes presented by chef Kim Byeong-jin, who emphasizes the original flavors of ingredients through in-depth research into Korean cooking. Its signature dish of braised abalones, made with soft abalones and soy sauce aged 10 years, is especially praised by customers.

Address	서울시 강남구 도산대로 317, M층 Floor M, 317, Dosan-daero, Gangnam-gu, Seoul
Tel	02-545-9845
Menu	온날 코스 Onnal Course ₩130,000-169,000 가온 코스 Gaon Course ₩260,000
Hours	화·수요일 Tuesday & Wednesday 17:00-22:00 목-토요일 Thursday-Saturday 12:00-14:30, 17:00-22:00 일·월요일 휴무 Closed on Sundays & Mondays
	gaon_seoul

한식 | Korean

권숙수 한식 Korean
Kwonsooksoo

권우중 셰프가 직접 담근 장과 식초, 김치와 장아찌 등을 활용해 품격 있는 한식 파인 다이닝을 선보인다. 전국 각지의 귀한 식재료를 발굴하고 창의적으로 담아내는 셰프의 열정이 돋보인다. 코스의 모든 요리는 개인 반상으로 서브된다.

Kwonsooksoo presents Korean fine dining using Korean sauces, vinegar, and kimchi prepared by chef Kwon Woo-joong. This enthusiastic chef shows his passion with top-quality ingredients from all over the country in creative dishes. All course dishes are served individually to each customer.

Address	서울시 강남구 압구정로80길 37 37, Apgujeong-ro 80-gil, Gangnam-gu, Seoul
Tel	02-542-6268
Menu	런치 코스 Lunch Course ₩160,000 디너 코스 Dinner Course ₩260,000
Hours	12:00-15:00, 18:00-22:30 일·월요일 휴무 Closed on Sundays & Mondays
	kwonsooksoo

꽃, 밥에 피다 전통 한식 Traditional Korean
A Flower Blossom on the Rice

친환경 급식 기업에서 운영하는 식당으로 믿을 만한 생산자와 협업해 건강한 밥상을 차려낸다. 유기농 친환경 식재료와 전통 장으로 맛을 내며, 현미찹쌀밥과 오색 나물을 달걀지단으로 감싼 뒤 식용 꽃으로 마무리한 보자기 비빔밥이 대표 메뉴다.

A Flower Blossom on the Rice, run by an eco-friendly food service provider, serves healthy dishes in collaboration with trustworthy ingredient producers. The restaurant uses eco-friendly organic ingredients and traditional Korean sauces. Its signature dish is Bojagi Bibimbap (Bibimbap Wrapped in Omelet), with sticky brown rice and five-color salad wrapped in egg, and an edible flower on top.

Address 서울시 종로구 인사동16길 3-6
  3-6, Insadong 16-gil, Jongno-gu, Seoul
Tel 02-732-0276
Menu 보자기 비빔밥 세트 Bojagi Bibimbap Set ₩25,000
  비건 코스 완전 소중한 꽃밥 Vegan Course Precious Flower Rice ₩45,000
Hours 11:30-15:00, 17:30-21:00
  명절 당일 휴무 Closed on Lunar New Year's Day and Chuseok
  flowerrice_official

한식 | Korean

^{NEW}
남도제철맛집 전통 한식 Traditional Korean
Nam Do Jecheol

전라남도의 제철 해산물을 맛깔스럽게 선보이는 한정식 전문 업장이다. 흑산도 홍어는 산지 직송으로 받아 2개월 이상 냉장 숙성시킨다. 봄엔 병어와 뻘낙지, 여름엔 민어와 덕자 등 서울에서 쉽게 맛보기 힘든 해산물을 회, 무침, 조림 등으로 내온다.

Nam Do Jecheol serves delicious Korean table d'hôte made with seasonal seafood of Jeollanam-do. Skates are directly delivered from Heuksando Island and cold-aged for at least two months. You can taste hard-to-find seasonal seafoods such as silver pomfret and mud flat octopus in the spring and croaker and butterfish in the summer. The restaurant serves different types of raw fish, raw fish salad, and braised fish.

Address	서울시 영등포구 양평로24길 9, 107동 상가 107, 9, Yangpyeong-ro 24-gil, Yeongdeungpo-gu, Seoul
Tel	02-2672-5955
Menu	흑산도 홍어 (250g) Heuksan Skate (250g) ₩80,000 민어 (250g) Croaker (250g) ₩100,000
Hours	12:30-13:30, 16:00-22:00 일요일 휴무 Closed on Sundays

한식 | Korean

라연 한식 Korean
La Yeon

신라호텔의 한식 파인 다이닝으로, <라연>의 전신인 <서라벌> 시절부터 30년 넘게 몸담아온 김성일 총괄 셰프가 주방을 이끈다. 전국의 고급 제철 식재료를 활용한 기품 있는 코스에 세심한 서비스가 더해져 멋진 식사 경험을 선사한다.

La Yeon is a Korean fine dining restaurant in The Shilla Seoul hotel led by head chef Kim Sung-il, who has been working for the restaurant for over 30 years since the time of La Yeon's predecessor, "Seorabeol." The restaurant offers elegant meal courses made with premium seasonal ingredients, providing an elaborate meal experience along with delicate service.

Address	서울시 중구 동호로 249, 서울신라호텔 23층
	23F, The Shilla Seoul, 249, Dongho-ro, Jung-gu, Seoul
Tel	02-2230-3367
Menu	점심 코스 Lunch Course ₩175,000
	저녁 코스 Dinner Course ₩270,000
Hours	12:00-14:30, 17:30-21:30
Ⓦ	www.shilla.net

레스토랑 주은 한식 Korean
Restaurant Jueun

경희궁 뒤편 고즈넉한 골목에 자리 잡은 공간에서 <한식공간> 출신 박주은 총괄 셰프가 계절을 담은 한식을 코스로 풀어낸다. 통영의 도다리쑥국을 쑥도다리 편수로 재해석하는 등 신선한 시각이 돋보인다. 명장이 만든 그릇들도 한식의 미를 더한다.

Restaurant Jueun is situated in the peaceful alleyway at the back of Gyeonghuigung Palace. Head chef Park Ju-eun, who used to work for Hansikgonggan, presents seasonal Korean course meals. The dishes show the head chef's creativity, including Tongyeong mugwort soup with ridged-eye flounder reinterpreted as a mandu soup. Dishes made by a master artisan enhance the beauty of Korean cuisine.

Address	서울시 종로구 경희궁길 36, 8층 8F, 36, Gyeonghuigung-gil, Jongno-gu, Seoul
Tel	02-540-8580
Menu	점심 코스 Lunch Course ₩120,000-200,000 저녁 코스 Dinner Course ₩200,000
Hours	화-목요일 Tuesday-Thursday 17:30-22:00 금·토요일 Friday & Saturday 12:00-15:00, 18:00-22:00 일·월요일 휴무 Closed on Sundays & Mondays
	jueun_restaurant

한식 | Korean

마포옥 전통 한식 Traditional Korean
Mapo-ok

1949년부터 그 명맥을 이어와 서울시 미래유산으로 지정된 설렁탕 노포다. 마포식 설렁탕은 맑은 국물이 특징. 사골을 넣고 푹 고아낸 진한 국물에 두툼한 양지머리를 푸짐하게 얹어 낸다. 직접 담근 겉절이, 깍두기 등의 김치 맛도 일품.

Mapo-ok is a long-established restaurant serving ox bone soup, having first opened its doors in 1949, that has been designated as a Seoul Future Heritage. Mapo ox bone soup features a distinctly clear broth. Ox bones are simmered over a long time to make a strong broth. The soup is served with thick-sliced beef brisket. The restaurant's own fresh kimchi and diced radish kimchi are popular as well.

Address 서울시 마포구 토정로 312
312, Tojeong-ro, Mapo-gu, Seoul
Tel 02-716-6661
Menu 양지 설렁탕 Beef Brisket and Ox Bone Soup ₩16,000
차돌탕 Thin Sliced Beef Brisket Soup ₩27,000
Hours 07:00-21:00
명절 당일 휴무 Closed on Lunar New Year's Day and Chuseok

무궁화 한식 Korean
Mugunghwa

온화한 전통미가 담긴 한식을 선보이는 롯데호텔 내 한식 레스토랑이다. 제철 식재료를 십분 활용해 조선 궁중 요리를 현대에 맞게 재해석한다. 한식과 잘 어우러지는 43종의 와인 컬렉션을 비롯해 전통차 소믈리에의 티 페어링 서비스도 즐길 수 있다.

Mugunghwa is Lotte Hotel's Korean restaurant that presents the delicate beauty of Korean traditional dishes. The restaurant adds a modern twist to the Joseon dynasty's royal cuisine using seasonal ingredients. It features a collection of 43 wines that pair well with Korean dishes. You can also experience the tea pairing service from traditional tea sommeliers.

Address	서울시 중구 을지로 30, 롯데호텔서울 본관 38층 38F, Lotte Hotel Seoul Main Building, 30, Eulji-ro, Jung-gu, Seoul
Tel	02-317-7061
Menu	백록 Baek Rock ₩205,000 무궁화 Mugunghwa ₩280,000
Hours	11:30-14:30, 18:00-22:00
W	www.lottehotel.com

한식 | Korean

밍글스 모던 한식 Modern Korean
Mingles

한식을 기반으로 한 창작 요리를 선보이는 강민구 셰프의 파인 다이닝이다. 발효 채소와 장을 창의적으로 조합해 익숙하면서도 전혀 새로운 맛을 선보인다. 특히 된장, 간장, 고추장이 오묘하게 어우러진 '장 트리오'는 단골들에게 두고두고 회자되는 디저트.

Mingles is a fine dining restaurant run by owner chef Kang Min-goo, serving creative dishes based on Korean cuisine. The restaurant presents familiar but completely new tastes, combining fermented vegetables and Korean sauces in a creative way. In particular, its Jang Trio dessert dish, which shows the harmony of soybean paste, soy sauce, and red chili paste, is loved by its regular patrons.

Address 서울시 강남구 도산대로67길 19, 2층
2F, 19, Dosan-daero 67-gil, Gangnam-gu, Seoul
Tel 02-515-7306
Menu 런치 코스 Lunch Course ₩180,000
디너 코스 Dinner Course ₩280,000
Hours 12:00-15:00, 18:00-22:00
일요일 휴무 Closed on Sundays

mingles_restaurant

봉피양 방이점 전통 한식 Traditional Korean
Bon Pi Yang

한식벽제그룹에서 운영하는 평양냉면·갈비 전문점이다. 평양냉면은 한우와 돈육을 진하게 우려낸 육수의 육 향과 메밀 함량 80%인 면의 은은한 메밀 향이 천상 궁합을 이룬다. 1등급 한돈 목심에 비법 양념장을 더한 돼지本갈비의 명성도 높다.

Bon Pi Yang is a restaurant that specializes in Pyeongyang cold buckwheat noodles and grilled pork galbi, run by Hansik Byeok-je Group. Pyeongyang cold buckwheat noodles display the perfect harmony of a deep, rich broth of Korean beef and pork, and buckwheat noodles containing 80% buckwheat. The restaurant is also famous for grilled pork galbi made with Grade 1 Korean pork shoulder and its own secret sauce.

Address	서울시 송파구 양재대로71길 1-4(본관) Main Building, 1-4, Yangjae-daero 71-gil, Songpa-gu, Seoul
Tel	02-415-5527
Menu	돼지목심 本갈비 Grilled Pork Shoulder Galbi ₩33,000 평양냉면 Pyeongyang Cold Buckwheat Noodles ₩15,000
Hours	11:30–22:00
	byeokje_dining

한식 | Korean

비채나 모던 한식 Modern Korean
Bicena

잠실 롯데월드타워 81층에 위치해 서울이 한눈에 내려다보이는 절경과 함께 단아한 한식 코스를 즐길 수 있는 모던 한식당이다. 전광식 총괄 셰프가 잊어가는 향토 음식을 재해석해 코스로 풀어낸다. 노태정 소믈리에가 엄선한 와인 리스트도 이곳의 강점.

Bicena is a modern Korean restaurant located on the 81st floor of Lotte World Tower in Jamsil. You can enjoy an elegant Korean course meal while looking out across the beautiful full view of Seoul city. Head chef Jun Kwang-sik reinterprets and presents local Korean dishes in a course meal. The wine list selected by sommelier Roh Tae-jeong is also popular.

Address 서울시 송파구 올림픽로 300, 롯데월드타워 81층
81F, Lotte World Tower, 300, Olympic-ro, Songpa-gu, Seoul
Tel 02-3213-1261
Menu 점심 산천 코스 Lunch Sancheon Course
주중 Weekdays ₩95,000·주말 Weekends ₩120,000
저녁 일월 코스(평일) Ilwol Dinner Course (Weekdays) ₩185,000
Hours 11:30-14:30, 18:00-22:00
bicena_seoul

세븐스도어 모던 한식 Modern Korean
7th Door

김대천 셰프가 한식의 특징인 발효를 테마로 창작 요리를 선보이는 모던 한식 레스토랑이다. 길게는 10년 이상 직접 발효시키거나 명인과 협업한 산물들을 요리에 감각적으로 담아낸다. 마치 공연을 감상하듯 오픈 키친을 볼 수 있는 바 테이블도 특별하다.

In the modern Korean restaurant 7th Door, chef Kim Dae-chun presents creative dishes under the theme of fermentation, one of the distinctive features of Korean cuisine. He uses his own fermented ingredients aged up to ten years for his cooking along with other ingredients made by collaborating with masters. You can see the chefs cooking in the open kitchen from the bar table, like watching a show.

Address	서울시 강남구 학동로97길 41, 4층 4F, 41, Hakdong-ro 97-gil, Gangnam-gu, Seoul
Tel	010-9660-3011
Menu	런치 코스 Lunch Course 평일 Weekdays ₩150,000 · 주말 Weekends ₩180,000 디너 코스 Dinner Course ₩280,000
Hours	12:00-15:00, 18:00-22:00 일·월요일 휴무 Closed on Sundays & Mondays
◎	7thdoor_official

한식 | Korean

소설 한남 모던 한식 Modern Korean
SOSEOUL hannam

엄태철 셰프가 전통에 현대적인 상상력을 가미한 요리를 선보이는 모던 한식 레스토랑이다. 업장명엔 '한 편의 소설 같은 한식'과 '서울의 현재를 반영한다'는 의미가 담겼다. 코스에 무침, 지짐, 찜, 조림 등 다양한 한식 종류를 고르게 구성한 점도 돋보인다.

SOSEOUL hannam is a modern Korean restaurant where chef Eom Tae-cheol serves traditional Korean dishes augmented with modern imagination. Its name, SOSEOUL Hannam, means "Korean cuisine like a novel" and "showing the present time of Seoul." The meal courses consist of an even variety of Korean foods such as salad, pan-fried dishes, steamed dishes, and braised dishes.

Address 서울시 용산구 한남대로20길 21-18, B동 지하 1층
B1, Building B, 21-18, Hannam-daero 20-gil, Yongsan-gu, Seoul
Tel 02-797-5995
Menu 런치 코스 Lunch Course ₩110,000
디너 코스 Dinner Course ₩180,000
Hours 12:00-15:00, 18:00-22:00
월요일 휴무 Closed on Mondays

soseoul_hannam

스와니예 모던 한식 Modern Korean
SOIGNÉ

Ⓟ

이준 셰프의 정교한 '서울 퀴진'을 맛볼 수 있는 파인 다이닝이다. 전통과 현대, 다양한 문화가 뒤섞인 서울에서 영감을 얻어 분기별로 새로운 에피소드로 코스를 선보인다. 고조리서, 서양 미술사, 테루아, 감칠맛 등 그간 진행해온 에피소드만 27편이 넘는다.

SOIGNÉ is a fine dining restaurant where you can enjoy chef Lee Jun's delicate "Seoul cuisine." Inspired by Seoul, where tradition, modernity, and various cultures coexist, he presents new courses every quarter in a series of episodes. He has developed 27 episodes so far, including Old Recipes, Western Art History, Terroir, and Savory Flavor.

Address	서울시 서초구 반포대로39길 46, 지하 1층 B1, 46, Banpo-daero 39-gil, Seocho-gu, Seoul
Tel	02-3477-9386
Menu	런치 Lunch ₩125,000 디너 Dinner ₩210,000
Hours	12:00-15:00, 18:00-22:00 월·화요일 휴무 Closed on Mondays & Tuesdays
◎	soigneseoul

한식 | Korean

NEW
안씨 막걸리 한식 Korean
Mr. Ahn's Craft Makgeolli

전통적이면서도 모던한 감각의 한국 술집을 표방하는 곳이다. 한치 안에 돼지고기와 버섯 소를 채운 '한치순대', 여주 송고버섯과 마늘종 장아찌에 솔잎 훈연 향을 입힌 '버섯' 등 개성 넘치는 메뉴들이 엄선한 우리 술과 좋은 매칭을 이룬다.

Mr. Ahn's Craft Makgeolli is both a traditional and contemporary Korean bar. Its signature dishes include the Swordtip Squid Sundae, made of swordtip squid filled with pork and mushroom, and Mushrooms, made of pine needle-smoked Yeoju songgo mushroom and pickled garlic stem. Its unique dishes pair well with select Korean liquor.

Address	서울시 용산구 회나무로 3, 1층 1F, 3, Hoenamu-ro, Yongsan-gu, Seoul
Tel	010-5172-2229
Menu	한치순대 Swordtip Squid Sundae ₩30,000 줄무늬전갱이회 Sliced White Trevally ₩36,000
Hours	18:00–23:00
◎	ahn.mak

한식 | Korean

온지음 레스토랑 _{한식} Korean
ONJIUM

전통문화연구소 온지음에서 운영하는 한식 다이닝. 조선왕조 궁중음식 이수자 조은희 셰프와 박성배 셰프가 고조리서, 지역 반가에서 계승되는 조리법을 재현하는 데 그치지 않고, 새로운 재료를 접목해 현대적으로 계승한 요리를 선보인다.

This is a Korean restaurant run by the traditional culture research institute ONJIUM. Chef Jo Eun-hui, who completed the Joseon royal cuisine course, and chef Park Seong-bae have reinterpreted old recipes, recorded in ancient recipe books or handed down by local noble families, in a contemporary way by adding new ingredients.

Address 서울시 종로구 효자로 49, 4층
4F, 49, Hyoja-ro, Jongno-gu, Seoul
Tel 02-6952-0024
Menu 점심 코스 Lunch Course ₩140,000
저녁 코스 Dinner Course ₩220,000
Hours 12:00-15:00, 18:00-22:00
월요일·주말 휴무 Closed on Mondays & Weekends

onjium_restaurant

용수산 비원 전통 한식 Traditional Korean
Yong Su San

1980년도부터 개성 대갓집의 맛을 선보여온 한정식 전문 업장이다. 고려의 수도로서 명성을 떨쳤던 개성의 미식을 1대 최상옥 회장에 이어 허정유 대표가 3대째 잇고 있다. 개성 청포묵, 탕평채, 보쌈김치 등 10여 가지 요리가 코스로 나온다.

Yong Su San is a Korean table d'hôte restaurant that has been serving the dishes of wealthy families of Gaeseong since the 1980s. The first owner Choi Sang-ok opened the restaurant to continue the delicacies of Gaeseong, the capital city of the Goryeo dynasty, and now the third-generation owner Heo Jeong-yu is inheriting the legacy. Its meal courses consist of around ten dishes, including Gaeseong mung bean jelly salad, tangpyeong-chae, and wrapped kimchi.

Address	서울시 종로구 창덕궁1길 2 2, Changdeokgung 1-gil, Jongno-gu, Seoul
Tel	02-743-5999
Menu	궁정식(점심) Royal Palace Set Menu (Lunch) ₩97,000 예절정식(저녁) Courtesy Set Menu (Dinner) ₩148,000
Hours	11:30-15:00, 17:30-21:30 월요일 휴무 Closed on Mondays
◉	yongsusan_biwon

한식 | Korean

우래옥 전통 한식 Traditional Korean
Woo Lae Oak

서울에서 가장 오래된 평양냉면 전문점이다. 평양에서 유명한 냉면집 <명월관>을 운영하던 창업주 장원일이 월남해 1946년 을지로에 개업한 뒤 현재까지 이어져오고 있다. 툭툭 끊기는 메밀 면과 진한 육 향으로 1년 내내 문전성시를 이룬다.

Woo Lae Oak is the oldest Pyeongyang cold buckwheat noodles restaurant in Seoul. The first restaurant owner Jang Won-il, who previously ran "Myeongwolgwan", one of the most popular cold buckwheat noodles restaurants in Pyeongyang, defected to South Korea and opened this place in Eulji-ro in 1946. Its soft noodles and deep, rich broth are the reason that the restaurant is crowded with customers throughout the year.

Address 서울시 중구 창경궁로 62-29
62-29, Changgyeonggung-ro, Jung-gu, Seoul
Tel 02-2265-0151
Menu 평양냉면 Pyeongyang Cold Buckwheat Noodles ₩16,000
불고기 Bulgogi ₩37,000
Hours 11:30-21:30
월요일 휴무 Closed on Mondays

윤서울 모던 한식 Modern Korean
YUN SEOUL

모던 한식 코스와 전통주의 어우러짐을 만끽할 수 있는 김도윤 셰프의 다이닝이다. 우리 밀을 자가 제면해 구수한 향의 들기름 면과 업장에서 직접 숙성한 생선을 활용한 요리 등 익숙하면서도 참신한 느낌이 가득한 한식을 선보인다.

YUN SEOUL is chef Kim Do-yun's restaurant where you can enjoy the harmony of modern Korean cuisine and traditional liquor. The restaurant makes noodles with Korean wheat and perilla oil using their own recipe. They also age fish at the restaurant for even more delicious dishes, serving familiar but creative Korean dishes.

Address	서울시 마포구 홍익로2길 31, 1층 1F, 31, Hongik-ro 2-gil, Mapo-gu, Seoul
Tel	02-336-3323
Menu	런치 코스 Lunch Course ₩75,000 디너 코스 Dinner Course ₩120,000
Hours	수-토요일 Wednesday-Saturday 12:00-15:00, 18:30-21:00 일-화요일 휴무 Closed on Sundays through Tuesdays
◎	yunseoul_office

한식 | Korean

(NEW)
을밀대 전통 한식 Traditional Korean
Eul Mil Dae

이북 출신 창업주가 1971년 문을 연 평양냉면 전문점이다. 국내산 메밀로 주문 즉시 뽑아낸 면은 두껍고 거칠며, 육수는 황소 전체 부위와 각종 채소로 푹 끓여내 깊은 감칠맛을 지니고 있다. 특히 평양냉면 입문자에게 인기가 좋다.

Eul Mil Dae is a Pyeongyang cold buckwheat noodles restaurant opened by a North Korean defector in 1971. It makes noodles with Korean buckwheat as soon as an order is placed. Its buckwheat noodles are thick and rough, and they make a savory broth using all ox cuts and various vegetables. The restaurant is especially popular with people who are new to Pyeongyang cold buckwheat noodles.

Address	서울시 마포구 숭문길 24 24, Sungmun-gil, Mapo-gu, Seoul
Tel	02-717-1922
Menu	물냉면 Cold Buckwheat Noodles ₩13,000 회냉면 Cold Buckwheat Noodles with Raw Fish ₩17,000
Hours	11:00-22:00 명절 당일 휴무 Closed on Lunar New Year's Day and Chuseok
	eulmildae

NEW
이타닉 가든 모던 한식 Modern Korean
Eatanic Garden

강남 럭셔리 호텔 조선 팰리스 36층에 위치한 파인 다이닝이다. 손종원 셰프가 한식의 미학과 글로벌한 조리 스킬이 조화를 이루는 요리를 선보인다. 콜라비를 동치미처럼 발효시켜 다양한 식감으로 조리하는 등 맛의 섬세한 레이어가 돋보인다.

Eatanic Garden is a fine dining restaurant located on the 36th floor of Josun Palace, a luxurious hotel in Gangnam. Chef Son Jong-won serves harmonious dishes based on the aesthetic of Korean cuisine and his global cooking skills. The restaurant boasts delicate layers of flavor, including kohlrabi fermented with the method for radish water kimchi to create a variety of textures.

Address	서울시 강남구 테헤란로 231, 조선 팰리스 36층 36F, Josun Palace, 231 Teheran-ro, Gangnam-gu, Seoul
Tel	02-727-7610
Menu	런치 코스 Lunch Course ₩190,000 디너 코스 Dinner Course ₩320,000
Hours	12:00-14:30, 18:00-22:00 월요일 휴무 Closed on Mondays
◉	eatanicgarden

한식 | Korean

정식당 모던 한식 Modern Korean
JUNGSIKDANG

'뉴코리안'이라는 새로운 다이닝 장르를 개척한 임정식 셰프가 서울과 뉴욕에서 선보이는 한식 파인 다이닝이다. 익숙한 한식 메뉴를 기발한 아이디어로 재탄생시켜 색다른 미각적 경험을 선사한다. 불고기밥을 바삭한 김부각으로 감싼 김밥이 단연 인기 메뉴.

JUNGSIKDANG is a Korean fine dining restaurant located in Seoul and New York by chef Yim Jung-sik, who developed a new dining genre called "New Korean." He presents a new dining experience by reinterpreting familiar Korean dishes with his brilliant ideas. Gimbap made with bulgogi rice wrapped in crisp fried laver is the most popular dish of the restaurant.

Address	서울시 강남구 선릉로158길 11
	11, Seolleung-ro 158-gil, Gangnam-gu, Seoul
Tel	02-517-4654
Menu	런치 코스 Lunch Course ₩155,000
	디너 코스 Dinner Course ₩250,000
Hours	12:00-15:00, 17:30-22:00
	jungsik_inc

주옥 모던 한식 Modern Korean
Joo Ok

서울광장이 시원하게 조망되는 더 플라자 호텔 3층에 위치한 신창호 셰프의 모던 코리안 다이닝이다. 제철 식재료와 발효 양념으로 한국적인 맛을 만들어낸다. 특히 직접 담근 천연 발효 식초와 농사지은 들깨를 짜낸 들기름은 이곳만의 비법 재료.

Joo Ok is a modern Korean restaurant led by chef Shin Chang-ho, located on the third floor of The Plaza Hotel Seoul where you can enjoy the wide view of Seoul Plaza while enjoying a meal. The restaurant presents Korean flavors with seasonal ingredients and fermented sauces. In particular, its own specially made, naturally fermented vinegar and perilla oil are the secrets to their dishes.

Address	서울시 중구 소공로 119, 더 플라자 호텔 3층 3F, The Plaza Hotel Seoul, 119 Sogong-ro, Jung-gu, Seoul
Tel	010-4461-1193
Menu	주옥 점심 코스 Joo Ok Lunch Course ₩140,000 주옥 저녁 코스 Joo Ok Dinner Course ₩240,000
Hours	12:00-15:00, 18:00-21:30 월요일 휴무 Closed on Mondays
◎	joook_seoul

한식 | Korean

Asian
아시안

계향각
Gaehanggak

도림
TOH LIM

따뚱
DA DONG

미토우
Mitou

부다스벨리
Buddha's Belly

스시메르
SUSHI MER

진진
JinJin

코지마
KOJIMA

팔레드 신
Palais de Chine

플레이버 타운
FLAVOUR TOWN

NEW

계향각 중식 Chinese
Gaehanggak

배화여대 전통조리학과 교수인 신계숙 셰프가 이끄는 중국 요리 전문 식당으로, 청나라 고조리서에 기반한 청요리를 선보인다. 소홍주를 넣고 삼겹살을 장시간 끓인 동파육과 해삼과 족발을 버무린 해삼쥬스가 주력 메뉴이다.

Gaehanggak is a Chinese restaurant led by chef Shin Kye-sook, a professor at Baewha Women's University in the Department of Traditional Korean Cuisine. The restaurant serves dishes of the Qing dynasty based on Qing's ancient recipe books. Its signature dishes are Red Braised Pork Belly, made by simmering pork belly with shaoxing wine, and Braised Sea Cucumber and Pork, made with seasoned sea cucumber and pigs' feet.

Address	서울시 종로구 동숭길 86, 1층 1F, 86 Dongsung-gil, Jongno-gu, Seoul
Tel	02-3674-7770
Menu	동파육 Red Braised Pork Belly ₩88,000 해삼쥬스 Braised Sea Cucumber and Pork ₩180,000
Hours	11:30-15:00, 17:00-22:00 월요일 휴무 Closed on Mondays
	shinkyesook

아시안 | Asian

도림 중식 Chinese
TOH LIM

여경옥 총괄 셰프가 이끄는 롯데호텔서울의 중식당. 정교한 조리 기법을 토대로 식재료 본연의 맛을 잘 살렸다는 평을 받는 곳이다. 정통 광둥·베이징식 요리는 물론, 창의성을 가미한 수준 높은 중국 요리를 소개한다.

TOH LIM is a Chinese restaurant of Lotte Hotel Seoul, led by head chef Yeo Gyeong-ok. The restaurant is widely praised for its delicate cooking skill emphasizing the original flavors of the ingredients. It serves high-quality creative Chinese dishes as well as traditional Cantonese and Beijing dishes.

Address 서울시 중구 을지로 30, 롯데호텔서울 본관 37층
37F, Lotte Hotel Seoul Main Building, 30 Eulji-ro, Jung-gu, Seoull
Tel 02-317-7101
Menu 코스 메뉴 Course Menu
런치 Lunch ₩120,000-210,000, 디너 Dinner ₩160,000-500,000
주말특선코스 Weekend Special Course ₩150,000-180,000
Hours 11:30-14:30, 18:00-22:00
Ⓦ www.lottehotel.com

따뚱 중식 Chinese
DA DONG

20년 이상 중국 현지에서 경력을 쌓은 셰프의 손맛을 느낄 수 있는 더 리버사이드 호텔 내 중식당이다. 참나무 화덕을 활용한 정통 방식의 베이징덕은 별미 중 별미. 이 밖에도 다금바리, 오골계, 자연송이 등 산해진미가 포함된 고급스러운 중식 요리를 식재료 본연의 맛을 살려 내놓는다.

In this Chinese restaurant of The Riverside Hotel Seoul, you can enjoy Chinese dishes made by the chef who built his culinary career in China for over 20 years. One of the most popular dishes is traditional Beijing duck baked in an oak-fired oven. The restaurant serves premium Chinese dishes made with all sorts of delicacies such as abalone, saw-edged perch, silky chicken, and wild pine mushrooms, emphasizing the original flavors of the quality ingredients.

Address	서울시 서초구 강남대로107길 6, 더 리버사이드 호텔 본관 2층 2F, The Riverside Hotel Seoul Main Building, 6, Gangnam-daero 107-gil, Seocho-gu, Seoul
Tel	02-6710-1888
Menu	베이징덕(북경오리) Beijing Duck ₩120,000 셰프 스페셜 코스(불도장·샥스핀 포함 코스) Chef's Special Course (including Buddha's Temptation Soup and Shark Fin) ₩125,000
Hours	11:30-15:00, 17:30-22:00
W	www.riversidehotel.co.kr

아시안 | Asian

미토우 일식 Japanese
Mitou

권영운, 김보미 셰프가 정교한 가이세키 오마카세를 펼친다. 완성도 높은 요리를 위해 계절에 따라 바뀌는 제철 재료를 적극 활용한다. 딸기를 곁들인 튀긴 참돔부터 오리 가슴살과 잎새버섯을 곁들인 오완에 이르기까지, 맛과 멋을 모두 살린 요리가 미감을 자극한다.

Chef Kwon Young-woon and Kim Bo-mi present the finest kaiseki omakase. The restaurant uses seasonal ingredients as much as possible to present top-quality dishes. Its delicious and beautiful dishes captivate the taste buds, such as Deep-Fried Sea Bream decorated with strawberry and Owan topped with duck breast and maitake mushroom.

Address	서울시 강남구 도산대로70길 24, 1층 1F, 24, Dosan-daero 70-gil, Gangnam-gu, Seoul
Tel	010-7286-9914
Menu	단일 코스 Single Course ₩220,000
Hours	18:00-22:00 월요일 휴무, 월 2회 일요일 휴무 Closed on Mondays and twice a month on Sundays
	mitouseoul

부다스벨리 타이 Thai
Buddha's Belly

[NEW]

태국 정부가 인증한 타이 전문 레스토랑이다. 주방 인원 모두가 태국 요리사들로 구성되어 현지의 맛을 그대로 느낄 수 있다. 게살과 각종 채소를 커리에 볶은 뿌님팟퐁 커리, 매운 칠리 소스와 바질이 어우러진 타이 파스타 등 이국적인 메뉴가 돋보인다.

Buddha's Belly is a Thai restaurant certified by the Thai government. The kitchen staff are all from Thailand, serving authentic Thai dishes. The restaurant features exotic dishes such as Poo Nim Pad Pong Garee (stir-fried crab and vegetable curry) and Thai Pasta seasoned with spicy chili sauce and basil.

Address	서울시 용산구 녹사평대로40길 48 48, Noksapyeong-daero 40-gil, Yongsan-gu, Seoul
Tel	1666-2753
Menu	뿌님팟퐁 커리 Poo Nim Pad Pong Garee M ₩26,400, L ₩34,100 타이 파스타 Thai Pasta ₩17,600
Hours	11:30-15:30, 16:30-22:00
	buddhasbelly_official

아시안 | Asian

스시메르 일식 Japanese
SUSHI MER

해비치 호텔앤드리조트가 운영하는 하이엔드급 스시 레스토랑이다. 이동수 셰프가 전국 산지에서 최상급 해산물을 공수해 수준 높은 오마카세 스시를 선보인다. 샴페인을 비롯해 프리미엄 사케, 소주 등 스시와 페어링하기 좋은 주류 리스트도 충실하다.

SUSHI MER is a high-end sushi restaurant run by Haevichi Hotel & Resort. Chef Lee Dong-su serves premium omakase sushi dishes made with high-quality seafood brought from all over the country. The restaurant offers a wide range of liquors that pair with sushi, including champagne, premium sake, and soju.

Address	서울시 종로구 우정국로 26, 센트로폴리스 2층 2F, Centropolis, 26, Ujeongguk-ro, Jongno-gu, Seoul
Tel	02-722-4330
Menu	런치 Lunch ₩120,000 디너 Dinner ₩200,000
Hours	12:00-15:00, 18:00-22:00 일요일 휴무 Closed on Sundays
	haevichidining

진진 중식 Chinese
JinJin

호텔 중식 요리의 대중화를 이끈 왕육성 셰프의 중식당이다. 수준 높은 멘보샤와 싱싱한 활어를 쪄낸 칭찡우럭이 대표 메뉴로 손꼽힌다. 오향냉채, 깐풍기, 마파두부 등 정통 중식의 문턱을 낮춘 합리적인 가격대의 메뉴를 두루 만나볼 수 있다.

JinJin is a Chinese restaurant run by chef Wang Yuk-sung, who led the popularization of Chinese cuisine in Korean hotel industry. Its signature dishes are Menbosha and Steamed Chingjjing Rockfish using fresh fish. You can enjoy authentic Chinese dishes at reasonable prices, such as Five-Spice Chilled Salad, Sweet and Spicy Chicken, and Spicy Bean Curd.

Address	서울시 마포구 잔다리로 123 123, Jandari-ro, Mapo-gu, Seoul
Tel	070-5035-8878
Menu	멘보샤 Menbosha ₩25,000, 회원가 Members ₩20,000 칭찡우럭 Steamed Chingjjing Rockfish ₩39,000, 회원가 Members ₩31,200
Hours	12:00-15:00, 17:00-22:00
Ⓦ	www.jinjinseoul.modoo.at

아시안 | Asian

코지마 일식 Japanese
KOJIMA

일본 현지의 최상급 스시야와 견줄 만하다고 평가받는 박경재 셰프의 스시 오마카세 레스토랑이다. 최상급 자연산 재료만을 고집하며, 정통 방식으로 군더더기 없는 스시 메뉴를 선보인다. <아리아께> 시절부터 찾아오는 단골 고객이 늘 줄을 잇는 곳.

KOJIMA is a sushi omakase restaurant led by chef Park Kyung-jae, known to be comparable to high-end sushi restaurants in Japan. The restaurant presents top-quality sushi dishes using only premium natural ingredients and following authentic recipes. The restaurant is always crowded with its regulars who have been visiting since its predecessor, "Ariake."

Address	서울시 강남구 압구정로60길 21, 6층 6F, 21, Apgujeong-ro 60-gil, Gangnam-gu, Seoul
Tel	02-2056-1291
Menu	런치 오마카세 Lunch Omakase ₩220,000 디너 오마카세 Dinner Omakase ₩420,000
Hours	12:00-14:30, 18:30-22:00 일·월요일 휴무 (주말·공휴일 디너 18:00 오픈) Closed on Sundays & Mondays (Open from 6 p.m. on weekends and holidays)

팔레드신 중식 Chinese
Palais de Chine

레스케이프 호텔의 중식 레스토랑으로, 홍콩의 모던 차이니스 레스토랑 <모트32>의 노하우와 철학을 담은 광동식 메뉴를 선보인다. 셰프만의 노하우로 화덕에 구워내 바삭한 껍질과 촉촉한 속살이 일품인 '북경 오리'가 시그너처 메뉴다.

Palais de Chine, a Chinese restaurant in L'Escape Hotel, serves Cantonese dishes featuring the know-how and philosophy of Hong Kong's modern Chinese restaurant "Mott 32." The signature dish Beijing Duck, cooked by brazier with the chef's own recipe, has juicy meat and crispy skin.

Address	서울시 중구 퇴계로 67, 레스케이프 호텔 6층 6F, L'Escape Hotel, 67, Toegye-ro, Jung-gu, Seoul
Tel	02-317-4001
Menu	북경 오리 Beijing Duck ₩150,000 소흥주 칠리새우 Shaoxing Wine Chili Shrimp ₩48,000
Hours	07:00-10:00, 11:30-15:00, 17:30-22:00
	lescape_hotel

아시안 | Asian

플레이버 타운 중식 Chinese
FLAVOUR TOWN

세계 곳곳에서 내공을 다진 티케이, 클레어 셰프가 운영하는 아시안 다이닝. 족발튀김과 황제커리 등 독창적인 퓨전 중식을 선보인다. XO 바지락 누들, 시추안 닭찜 등의 개성 강한 메뉴가 가득하다.

This Asian restaurant is run by chefs TK and Clare, who have built their careers all over the world. The restaurant serves its own original fusion dishes such as Deep Fried Pigs' Feet and Emperor's Curry. You can find its variety of unique dishes including XO Clam Noodles and Sichuan Braised Chicken.

Address	서울시 성동구 서울숲4길 18-7 18-7, Seoulsup 4-gil, Seongdong-gu, Seoul
Tel	02-469-9954
Menu	족발튀김 Deep Fried Pigs' Feet ₩18,000 황제커리 Emperor's Curry 반 마리 Half ₩53,000, 한 마리 Whole ₩100,000
Hours	17:00-22:00 토요일 Saturday 12:00-15:00, 17:00-22:00 일·월요일 휴무 Closed on Sundays & Mondays
◉	flavourtownseoul

Western
양식

강민철 레스토랑
KANG MINCHUL Restaurant

구찌 오스테리아 서울
GUCCI OSTERIA SEOUL

기가스
GIGAS

더 그린테이블
The Green Table

디템포레
De tempore

라망 시크레
L'Amant Secret

레스토랑 알렌
Restaurant ALLEN

레스토랑 오와이
Restaurant OY

레스토랑 온
RESTAURANT ON

메종조
Maison Jo

모수 서울
MOSU

무오키
MUOKI

바위파스타바 한남
Bawipastabar

보르고 한남
BORGO HANNAM

보트르 메종
Votre Maison

비스트로 드 욘트빌
BISTROT de YOUNTVILLE

빈호
VINHO

셰로랑
Chez Laurent

알라 프리마
alla prima

에빗
EVETT

윌로뜨
Hulotte

임프레션
L'impression

제로컴플렉스
ZERO COMPLEX

캄포
Campo

페리지
PERIGEE

폴스다이너
Paul's Diner

강민철 레스토랑 <small>프렌치 French</small>
KANG MINCHUL Restaurant

세계적인 셰프 피에르 가니에르, 조엘 로부숑, 알랭 뒤카스의 레스토랑을 거친 강민철 셰프가 화려하고도 섬세한 터치가 가미된 프렌치 요리를 선보인다. 단 3개의 테이블이 있는 공간에서 프렌치 퀴진의 정수를 만끽할 수 있다.

Chef Kang Min-chul, who built his career at the restaurants of world-famous chefs such as Pierre Gagnaire, Joël Robuchon, and Alain Ducasse, serves French dishes augmented with a glamorous and delicate touch. The restaurant has only three tables, but it is enough to enjoy authentic French cuisine.

Address	서울시 강남구 도산대로68길 18, 지하 1층 B1, 18, Dosan-daero 68-gil, Gangnam-gu, Seoul
Tel	02-545-2511
Menu	런치 코스 Lunch Course ₩160,000 디너 코스 Dinner Course ₩320,000
Hours	12:00-14:30, 18:00-22:00 일·월요일 휴무 Closed on Sundays & Mondays

양식 | Western

구찌 오스테리아 서울 이탈리언 Italian
GUCCI OSTERIA SEOUL

이탈리아의 마시모 보투라 셰프와 구찌가 컬래버레이션한 전 세계 4번째 레스토랑. 셰프의 시그너처 메뉴를 포함해 로컬 재료를 활용한, 서울에서만 맛볼 수 있는 메뉴가 준비되어 있다. 직접 수확한 제철 채소와 이탈리아 모데나의 식재료가 조화롭게 어우러진다.

The world's fourth collaboration restaurant between Italian chef Massimo Bottura and GUCCI. The restaurant serves unique dishes that you can enjoy only in Seoul, including the chef's signature dishes made with local ingredients. You can experience the harmony of ingredients brought from Modena, Italy and seasonal vegetables harvested by chefs.

Address 서울시 용산구 이태원로 223, 6층
6F, 223, Itaewon-ro, Yongsan-gu, Seoul
Tel 02-795-1119
Menu 시그니처 테이스팅 7 코스 Signature Tasting 7-Course ₩170,000
가옥 테이스팅 5 코스 Gaok Tasting 5-Course ₩120,000
Hours 12:00-16:00, 18:00-22:00
guccriosteria

기가스 지중해식 Mediterranean
GIGAS

지속가능성을 추구하는 모던 지중해식 레스토랑이다. 오랫동안 유럽에서 일해온 정하완 셰프가 전통적인 지중해 요리를 모던하게 재해석해 선보인다. 사용하는 채소 대부분은 가족 농장에서 유기농으로 재배한 것으로, 진정한 팜투테이블을 실천하고 있다.

GIGAS is a modern Mediterranean restaurant that pursues sustainability. Chef Jung Ha-wan, who built his career in Europe over a long period of time, serves traditional Mediterranean dishes in a contemporary fashion. The restaurant is applying true farm-to-table practices, with most of the vegetables used cultivated organically at his own family farm.

Address	서울시 강남구 도산대로45길 8-7, 2층 2F, 8-7, Dosan-daero 45-gil, Gangnam-gu, Seoul
Tel	02-3448-9929
Menu	디너 코스 Dinner Course ₩130,000
Hours	18:00-22:30 일·월요일 휴무 Closed on Sundays & Mondays
◎	gigas_seoul

양식 | Western

더 그린테이블
The Green Table
코리안 프렌치 Korean French

제철 채소의 매력을 경험할 수 있는 김은희 셰프의 프렌치 레스토랑이다. 고조리서, 사찰 음식, 발효, 꽃과 허브 등 셰프의 관심사를 요리에 섬세하게 반영한다. 하나하나 직접 고른 국내 도예가의 식기가 고아한 담음새를 완성한다.

The Green Table is chef Kim Eun-hee's French restaurant where you can enjoy seasonal vegetables. She reflects her interests of ancient recipe books, temple food, fermentation, edible flowers, and herbs in her cooking in a delicate manner. She selected each piece of tableware, all made by Korean potters, for the best food plating and presentation.

Address	서울시 강남구 선릉로155길 13, 2층 2F, 13, Seolleung-ro 155-gil, Gangnam-gu, Seoul
Tel	02-591-2672
Menu	계절 런치 코스 Seasonal Lunch Course ₩120,000 계절 디너 코스 Seasonal Dinner Course ₩220,000
Hours	12:00-15:00, 18:00-22:00 (일요일 21:30까지) (Closed at 9:30 p.m. on Sunday) 월·화요일 휴무 Closed on Mondays & Tuesdays
	restaurant_thegreentable

디템포레 프렌치 French
De tempore

<렁팡스>와 <보이어>로 성수동에서 큰 인기를 얻은 김태민 셰프가 한남동에 마련한 네오 비스트로 업장이다. 친숙한 재료의 색다른 조합이 돋보인다. 밝고 아늑한 공간에서 프렌치 코스 요리를 편안한 분위기에서 즐길 수 있다.

De tempore is a neo bistro in Hannam-dong by chef Kim Tae-min, who once led the popular restaurants "L'enfance" and "Boyer" in Seongsu-dong. The restaurant boasts unique combinations of familiar ingredients. You can enjoy a French course meal in a bright, cozy dining space.

Address	서울시 용산구 한남대로 37 37, Hannam-daero, Yongsan-gu, Seoul
Tel	070-4848-6359
Menu	런치 코스 Lunch Course ₩65,000 디너 코스 Dinner Course ₩105,000
Hours	12:00-15:00, 18:00-22:30 일·월요일 휴무 Closed on Sundays & Mondays
	detempore_neobistro

양식 | Western

라망시크레 프렌치 French
L'Amant Secret

레스케이프 호텔의 모던 프렌치 레스토랑이다. 미국 유수의 레스토랑에서 경험을 쌓은 손종원 셰프가 프렌치 테크닉을 기반으로 로컬 식재료를 활용한 '서울 퀴진'을 선보인다. '비밀 연인'이라는 상호처럼 로맨틱한 분위기의 공간도 강점.

L'Amant Secret is a modern French restaurant in L'Escape Hotel. Chef Son Jong-won, who built his career in prominent restaurants in the United States, offers creative "Seoul cuisine" made with local ingredients based on his French cooking skills. Like the name of the restaurant, meaning "a secret lover", its romantic interior design is a special charm.

Address	서울시 중구 퇴계로 67, 레스케이프 호텔 26층 26F, L'Escape Hotel, 67, Toegye-ro, Jung-gu, Seoul
Tel	02-317-4003
Menu	라망시크레 런치 L'Amant Secret Lunch ₩130,000 라망시크레 디너 L'Amant Secret Dinner ₩200,000
Hours	12:00-15:00, 18:00-22:00 일요일 휴무 Closed on Sundays
	lamant_secret

양식 | Western

레스토랑 알렌 모던 프렌치 Modern French
Restaurant ALLEN

서현민 셰프의 영어 이름을 내건 컨템퍼러리 다이닝. 근간이 되는 프렌치 오트 퀴진에 제철 식재료와 발효, 숙성 등의 조리 기법을 접목했다. 더불어 평창에 유기농 농장을 운영하며 건강한 식재료의 다양화에 힘쓰고 있다.

This is a contemporary dining restaurant named after chef Suh Hyun-min's English name. Seasonal ingredients and cooking skills such as fermentation and aging are added to French haute cuisine, which is the basis of the restaurant. The restaurant is running an organic farm in Pyeongchang to diversify its healthy ingredients.

Address	서울시 강남구 테헤란로 231, E205호 E205, 231, Teheran-ro, Gangnam-gu, Seoul
Tel	02-6985-7214
Menu	런치 테이스팅 코스 Lunch Tasting Course ₩150,000 디너 테이스팅 코스 Dinner Tasting Course ₩260,000
Hours	12:00-15:00, 18:00-22:00 일·월요일 휴무 Closed on Sundays & Mondays
	restaurant_allen

레스토랑 오와이 프렌치 French
Restaurant O Y

부부 중 오세훈 셰프가 요리를, 윤아영 셰프가 디저트를 담당하는 프렌치 레스토랑으로, 제철 식재료를 활용해 프렌치 코스를 선보인다. 복잡한 테크닉보다는 심플한 조리법으로 재료 본연의 맛과 향을 전하는 데 집중하고 있다.

At this French restaurant run by a married chef couple, chef Oh Se-hun cooks meal dishes and chef Yoon Ah-young prepares desserts, serving French courses using seasonal ingredients. They focus on presenting the original flavors and aromas of the ingredients with simple recipes rather than using complicated cooking techniques.

Address	서울시 강남구 선릉로148번길 48-12, 지하 1층 B1, 48-12, Seolleung-ro 148-gil, Gangnam-gu, Seoul
Tel	02-515-7250
Menu	런치 코스 Lunch Course ₩85,000 디너 코스 Dinner Course ₩180,000
Hours	12:00-15:00, 18:00-22:00 일·월요일 휴무 Closed on Sundays & Mondays
	restaurant_oy

양식 | Western

레스토랑 온 프렌치 French
RESTAURANT ON

유행을 좇기보다 고객의 취향에 집중하며 자신만의 요리 철학을 고수하는 김준형 셰프의 프렌치 레스토랑. 고객과 소통하며 온기 있는 요리를 준비한다. 프라이빗하게 구성된 여유 있는 공간에서 요리와 대화에 더욱 집중할 수 있다.

It is chef Kim Jun-hyeong's French restaurant that pursues his own cooking philosophy and focuses on customers' tastes, instead of following the trends. He serves heart-warming dishes while communicating with customers. You can focus on the quality dishes and conversation in a cozy and private space.

Address	서울시 강남구 도산대로92길 42, 지하 1층 B1, 42, Dosan-daero 92-gil, Gangnam-gu, Seoul
Tel	02-547-0467
Menu	코스 B Course B ₩132,000 최상위 코스 C Top Premium Course C ₩165,000
Hours	12:00-14:30, 18:00-22:00 월요일 휴무 Closed on Mondays
	restaurant_on

메종조 프렌치 French
Maison Jo

NEW

프랑스 현지의 맛을 전하는 프렌치 캐주얼 다이닝 공간이다. 조우람 샤퀴티에는 샤퀴테리를, 이은희 파티시에는 구움 과자와 빵을 만들며 부부가 함께하고 있다. 델리 형태로 운영되지만 요청하면 샌드위치나 샐러드를 와인과 간단히 즐길 수 있다.

Maison Jo is a French casual restaurant that presents French local dishes, run by a married chef couple. Charcutier Jo Woo-ram makes charcuterie, and pâtissier Lee Eun-hui bakes petits fours and bread. Although the restaurant is operated like a deli, you can enjoy a simple spread of sandwiches, salad, and wine upon request.

Address	서울시 서초구 반포대로7길 35, 1층 1F, 35, Banpo-daero 7-gil, Seocho-gu, Seoul
Tel	010-3926-4443
Menu	잠봉 뵈르 Jambon-Beurre ₩7,500 깜빠뉴 Campagne ₩7,000
Hours	12:00-16:00, 17:30-20:00 월·화요일 휴무 Closed on Mondays & Tuesdays
◉	maison_jo_

양식 | Western

모수 서울 이노베이티브 Innovative
MOSU

미국 샌프란시스코에서 시작해 최근 홍콩까지 진출한 안성재 셰프의 파인 다이닝이다. 아시안 테크닉에 프렌치 플레이팅, 한식 발효를 혼합한 혁신적인 퀴진을 선보인다. 재료를 저며 말리거나, 누룩을 띄워 섬세한 맛을 끌어내는 기술이 돋보인다.

It is a fine dining restaurant by chef Ahn Sung-jae, who started his cooking career in San Francisco of the United States and has recently expanded his business to Hong Kong. The restaurant presents innovative dishes by combining Asian cooking techniques, French-style plating, and Korean fermentation. His delicate cooking skills such as drying thin-sliced ingredients and fermenting malt upgrade the quality of the dishes.

Address	서울시 용산구 이태원로55가길 45 45, Itaewon-ro 55ga-gil, Yongsan-gu, Seoul
Tel	02-793-5995
Menu	런치 코스 Lunch Course ₩180,000 디너 코스 Dinner Course ₩320,000
Hours	12:00-15:00, 18:00-22:30 일·월요일 휴무 Closed on Sundays & Mondays
	mosuseoul

무오키
모던 프렌치 Modern French
MUOKI

미국, 영국, 호주, 남아프리카 공화국 등 세계 각지의 주방을 경험한 박무현 셰프의 컨템퍼러리 다이닝이다. 다양한 경험과 실험 정신을 바탕으로 창의적인 코스를 선보인다. 예상치 못한 식감과 맛의 조화를 선사하는 것이 셰프의 특기다.

You will encounter a contemporary dining experience by chef Park Moo-hyun, who built his career all over the world, including the United States, the UK, Australia and South Africa. The chef presents creative courses based on his wide range of experience and experimental spirit. He offers an experience of the harmony of unexpected textures and tastes.

Address	서울시 강남구 학동로55길 12-12, 2층 2F, 12-12, Hakdong-ro 55-gil, Gangnam-gu, Seoul
Tel	010-2948-4171
Menu	런치 코스 Lunch Course ₩100,000 디너 코스 Dinner Course ₩190,000
Hours	12:00-15:00, 18:00-22:00 일요일 휴무 Closed on Sundays

바위파스타바 이탤리언 Italian
Bawipastabar

생면 파스타 바 열풍의 출발점 격 업장으로, 한남동의 새로운 공간에서 진일보한 코스 메뉴를 선보인다. 식재료 상황에 따라 매달 조금씩 바뀌는 파스타와 안티파스토(전채), 그리고 소믈리에 추천 와인을 즐길 수 있다.

Bawipastabar is regarded as the starting point of the trend in raw noodle pasta bars in Korea. The restaurant presents high-quality course meals in a new space in Hannam-dong. The pastas and antipasti (first course dishes) slightly change every month depending on the ingredients. You can also enjoy wine recommended by a sommelier.

Address	서울시 용산구 이태원로 254, 지하 2층 B2, 254, Itaewon-ro, Yongsan-gu, Seoul
Menu	8코스 디너 8-Course Dinner ₩85,000
Hours	17:00–22:30 일·월요일 휴무 Closed on Sundays & Mondays
	bawipastabar

양식 | Western

보르고 한남 이탤리언 Italian
BORGO HANNAM

국내 유명 호텔의 총주방장을 거친 스테파노 디 살보 셰프가 이탈리아 각지의 퀴진을 재해석해 차려낸다. '마을'을 뜻하는 업장명처럼 아늑한 분위기가 특징. 그날의 추천 메뉴를 7코스로 선보이는 '셰프 테이블'이 별도 마련되어 있다.

Chef Stefano di Salvo, who has served as the head chef at famous Korean hotels, presents Italian dishes of different regions. As with the name of the restaurant, meaning "a small village", the restaurant features a cozy atmosphere. At Chef Table, you can enjoy the daily special menu in a seven-course meal.

Address	서울시 용산구 이태원로54길 31, 3층 3F, 31, Itaewon-ro 54-gil, Yongsan-gu, Seoul
Tel	02-6082-2727
Menu	오라타 Orata ₩25,000 칼다로 Caldaro ₩38,000
Hours	17:00-22:00 월요일 휴무 Closed on Mondays
〇	borgo_hannam

보트르 메종 _{프렌치} French
Votre Maison

파리 르 코르동 블루를 졸업한 국내 1세대 프렌치 셰프 박민재가 본질에 충실한 프렌치 요리를 코스로 선보인다. 화사하고 여유로운 다이닝 공간에서 섬세한 맛과 식감의 조합을 경험할 수 있다.

Chef Park Min-jae, the first-generation French chef who graduated from Le Cordon Bleu of Paris, serves French course meals focusing on the basics. You can experience the harmony of delicate flavors and textures in a bright and cozy dining hall.

Address	서울시 강남구 도산대로 420, B동 224호 224, Building B, 420, Dosan-daero, Gangnam-gu, Seoul
Tel	02-549-3800
Menu	런치 시그니처 코스 Lunch Signature Course ₩85,000-135,000 디너 시그니처 코스 Dinner Signature Course ₩185,000
Hours	12:00-15:00, 18:00-22:00 월·화요일 휴무 Closed on Mondays & Tuesdays
	votre__maison

양식 | Western

비스트로 드 욘트빌 프렌치 French
BISTROT de YOUNTVILLE

타미 리 셰프의 정통 프렌치 비스트로. 파리 현지의 비스트로를 연상시키는 고풍스러운 공간에서 클래식한 요리와 일상 속의 작은 휴식을 선사한다. 한때 셰프가 일했던 <프렌치 론드리>가 위치한 캘리포니아의 작은 마을 이름이 업장명이다.

It is an authentic French bistro by chef Tommie Lee. The elegant dining hall, reminiscent of local bistros in Paris, lets you enjoy a peaceful break with classic dishes. The restaurant was named after a small village in California where the chef's old workplace, "The French Laundry", is located.

Address 서울시 강남구 선릉로158길 13-7
13-7, Seolleung-ro 158-gil, Gangnam-gu, Seoul
Tel 02-541-1550
Menu 런치 클래식 4코스 Lunch Classic 4-Course ₩82,000
디너 트래디션 4코스 Dinner Tradition 4-Course ₩98,000
Hours 11:30-15:00, 18:00-22:00
yountvillebistro

빈호 이노베이티브 Innovative
VINHO

<밍글스> 출신의 김진호 소믈리에와 전성빈 셰프가 의기투합하여 오픈한 캐주얼 레스토랑이다. 동서양의 요소를 자유롭고 자연스럽게 결합한 요리와 페어링 와인을 서비스한다. 저녁에는 코스 요리, 심야에는 와인 바로 운영하고 있다.

VINHO is a casual restaurant jointly opened by sommelier Kim Jin-ho and chef Jeon Seong-bin, who used to work for "Mingles." The dishes combining both Eastern and Western elements are served with wine of the best pairing. The restaurant serves course meals for dinner and becomes a wine bar at night.

Address	서울시 강남구 학동로43길 38, 지상 162호 162, 38, Hakdong-ro 43-gil, Gangnam-gu, Seoul
Tel	010-9677-2302
Menu	디너 코스 Dinner Course ₩130,000 타르타르 Tartar ₩24,000
Hours	18:00-24:00 일·2, 4주 월요일 휴무 Closed on Sundays and every 2nd and 4th Monday
	restaurant.vinho

양식 | Western

셰로랑 프렌치 French
(구. 르 비스트로 남산)
Chez Laurent

항상 국내 거주 외국인들로 북적이는 프렌치 비스트로다. 프랑스에서 10년 넘게 외식업에 종사한 민병인 대표가 공간을 구상하고, 박영미 셰프가 주방을 책임진다. 프랑스 현지의 식사를 그대로 재현한 듯한 편안하고 따뜻한 요리가 기분을 북돋운다.

This French bistro is always crowded with foreign residents in Korea. The restaurant owner Min Byeong-in, previously engaged in food services in France for over 10 years, designed the interior and exterior, and chef Park Young-mi leads the kitchen. The authentic heart-warming French dishes will brighten up your day.

Address 서울시 용산구 신흥로 25, 1층
1F, 25, Sinheung-ro, Yongsan-gu, Seoul

Menu 오리 가슴살 스테이크와 포레스티에르 알감자
Duck Breast Steak & Potatoes Forestière ₩30,000대 range
광어 뫼니에르 Flatfish Meunière ₩35,000대 range

Hours 12:00-14:30, 18:00-23:00(화요일은 디너만 운영) (Dinner only on Tuesdays)
일·월요일 휴무 Closed on Sundays & Mondays

알라프리마 이노베이티브 Innovative
alla prima

대담하고 위트 넘치는 요리가 장점인 이노베이티브 다이닝. 일본에서 일식을 비롯해 프렌치, 이탈리언 등의 양식을 두루 경험한 김진혁 셰프가 그날그날의 상황에 맞춰 창의적인 코스 요리를 선보인다. 마치 연극 무대처럼 오픈 키친의 풍경을 감상할 수 있는 카운터 테이블이 인기다.

This innovative restaurant features bold and witty cuisines. Chef Kim Jin-hyuk, who built his cooking career in Japanese, French, and Italian cuisines in Japan, serves different creative course meals every day. The counter table is especially popular since you can see the cooking process in the open kitchen, like watching a performance while enjoying a meal.

Address	서울시 강남구 학동로 17길 13 13, Hakdong-ro 17-gil, Gangnam-gu, Seoul
Tel	02-511-2555
Menu	런치 코스 Lunch Course ₩130,000 디너 코스 Dinner Course ₩260,000
Hours	12:00-14:30, 18:00-22:00 화요일 휴무 Closed on Tuesdays
	restaurant_allaprima

양식 | Western

에빗 이노베이티브 Innovative
EVETT

호주 출신의 조셉 리저우드 셰프가 선보이는 이노베이티브 다이닝이다. 런던과 미국에서 쌓은 경험과 그만의 독특한 요리 철학으로 한식 재료를 재해석한 메뉴를 즐길 수 있다. 창의성과 실험적인 디자인, 활기 넘치는 서비스가 잊지 못할 미식 경험을 선사한다.

Chef Joseph Lidgerwood from Australia prepares the innovative dining. He reinterprets Korean ingredients based on his experience in London and the United States, and his unique cooking philosophy. A creative and experimental presentation of food and vibrant dining services give you an unforgettable gastronomic experience.

Address 서울시 강남구 도곡로 23길 33, 1층
1F, 33, Dogok-ro 23-gil, Gangnam-gu, Seoul
Tel 070-4231-1022
Menu 런치 코스 Lunch Course ₩120,000
디너 코스 Dinner Course ₩220,000
Hours 수-금요일 Wednesday-Friday 18:00-23:00
토·일요일 Saturday & Sunday 12:00-15:00, 18:00-23:00
월·화요일 휴무 Closed on Mondays & Tuesdays

restaurantevett

NEW

월로프 프렌치 French
Hulotte

자연주의 요리를 추구하는 이승준 셰프가 소금, 설탕, 버터의 사용을 최소화한 누벨 퀴진을 선보인다. 재료에서 뽑아낸 스톡과 쥐(Jus) 등으로 요리의 간을 완성한다. 레스토랑 근처에 마련한 작은 농장에서 약 20종의 허브를 직접 재배하여 사용하고 있다.

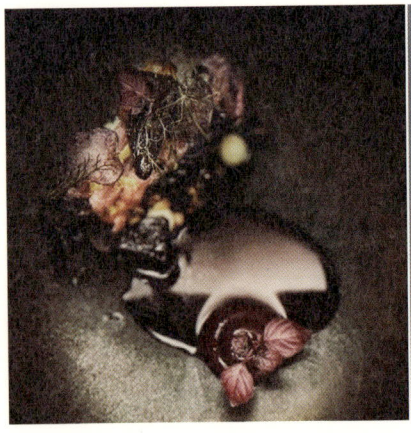

Chef Lee Seung-jun aims for naturalism to present nouvelle cuisine that minimizes the use of salt, sugar, and butter. He takes the stock and jus from ingredients and uses them for his cooking. Around 20 varieties of herbs for menus are cultivated at his farm near the restaurant.

Address	서울시 강남구 선릉로148길 48, 3층 3F, 48, Seolleung-ro 148-gil, Gangnam-gu, Seoul
Tel	02-722-0689
Menu	런치 코스 Lunch Course ₩130,000 디너 코스 Dinner Course ₩200,000
Hours	12:00-15:00, 18:00-22:00 월·화요일 휴무 Closed on Mondays & Tuesdays
	hulotte_seoul

양식 | Western

(NEW)
임프레션 이노베이티브 Innovative
L'impression

프렌치, 노르딕, 이탤리언, 호주 퀴진 등 윤태균 셰프의 경험이 녹아든 컨템퍼러리 다이닝. 채소와 해산물을 중심으로 계절의 맛을 표현한다. 야니스 페랄 소믈리에의 와인 페어링은 경험의 즐거움을 완성시켜주는 없어서는 안 될 요소다.

It is a contemporary dining restaurant run by chef Yoon Tae-gyun based on his experience in French, Nordic, Italian, and Australian cuisines. The restaurant presents seasonal flavors focusing on vegetables and seafood. You will not want to miss sommelier Yanis Feral's wine pairing service to complete your dining experience.

Address	서울시 강남구 언주로164길 24, 5층 5F, 24, Eonju-ro 164-gil, Gangnam-gu, Seoul
Tel	02-6925-5522
Menu	런치 코스 Lunch Course ₩140,000 디너 코스 Dinner Course ₩240,000
Hours	12:00-15:00, 18:00-22:00 일·월요일 휴무 Closed on Sundays & Mondays
	limpression_seoul

제로컴플렉스 이노베이티브 Innovative
ZERO COMPLEX

제철 재료, 특히 채소에서 많은 영감을 얻는다는 이충후 셰프의 실험실 같은 이노베이티브 다이닝이다. 특정한 형식에 얽매이기보다 재료 본연의 장점을 최대한으로 살려 요리를 완성한다. 화이트 톤 공간의 통창 너머로 전해지는 계절의 풍경과 요리의 제철 식재료가 멋진 조화를 이룬다.

It is an innovative laboratory-like dining restaurant of chef Lee Chung-hu, inspired by seasonal ingredients, particularly vegetables. The restaurant emphasizes the original character of ingredients as much as possible rather than adhering to a particular form. The seasonal ingredients harmonize well with the seasonal view through the window and the restaurant's white-toned interior design.

Address	서울시 중구 퇴계로 6가길 30, 3층 3F, 30, Toegye-ro 6ga-gil, Jung-gu, Seoul
Tel	02-532-0876
Menu	런치 코스 Lunch Course ₩120,000 디너 코스 Dinner Course ₩180,000
Hours	12:00-15:30, 18:00-22:30 월요일 휴무 Closed on Mondays
	zerocomplex_seoul

양식 | Western

캄포 이탈리언 Italian
Campo

일식 터치가 가미된 이탤리언 요리와 와인을 즐길 수 있는 소담한 공간으로, 임응규 셰프가 오래 살아온 명일동 골목에 자리하고 있다. 바지락 육수 베이스에 갈릭 오일과 성게알을 조합한 우니 파스타가 대표 메뉴다.

Campo is an adorable restaurant where you can enjoy some wine and Italian cuisine augmented with a touch of Japanese cuisine. The restaurant is located in an alleyway in Myeongil-dong where chef Lim Eung-gyu has been living for a long time. Its signature dish is Uni Pasta made with clam broth, garlic oil, and sea urchin roe.

Address	서울시 강동구 양재대로128길 41 41, Yangjae-daero 128-gil, Gangdong-gu, Seoul
Tel	010-4445-6608
Menu	우니 파스타 Uni Pasta ₩26,000 홍새우 Red Shrimp ₩23,000
Hours	18:00-24:00 일요일 휴무 Closed on Sundays
📷	campo_seoul

페리지 이탤리언 Italian
PERIGEE

클래식하고 섬세한 생면 파스타로 특히 젊은 층에게 압도적인 지지를 받고 있는 다이닝 공간이다. 미국에서 요리를 공부한 신가영, 임홍근 셰프 부부가 다양한 파스타를 선보인다. 라비올로, 피치, 안다리노스, 카바텔리 등의 다양한 면을 고유의 식감을 살려 준비한다.

Its classic and delicate raw noodle pasta is especially popular among younger generations. Chefs Shin Ga-young and Lim Hong-keun, a married couple who studied cooking in the United States, present a variety of pasta dishes. They use various types of pasta such as ravioli, pici, andarinos, and cavatelli.

Address	서울시 강남구 봉은사로68길 6-5, 1층 1F, 6-5, Bongeunsa-ro 68-gil, Gangnam-gu, Seoul
Menu	라자냐 Lasagna ₩32,000 안다리노스 Andarinos ₩36,000
Hours	17:00-22:00 일·월요일 휴무 Closed on Sundays & Mondays
◉	perigee_seoul

양식 | Western

폴스다이너 이탤리언 Italian
Paul's Diner

부부가 운영하는 해방촌의 작은 레스토랑. 유럽 내추럴 와인과 어울리는 이탈리아, 프랑스, 스페인 요리를 각 계절에 맞춰 준비한다. 특유의 편안하면서도 로맨틱한 분위기 덕에 단골손님의 발길이 끊이지 않는다.

It is a small restaurant in Haebangchon, run by a married couple. They serve different Italian, French, and Spanish dishes that go well with European natural wine, depending on the season. The restaurant is always loved by the regulars for its unique, cozy and romantic atmosphere.

Address	서울시 용산구 녹사평대로54길 6, 102호 102, 6, Noksapyeong-daero 54-gil, Yongsan-gu, Seoul
Tel	010-4045-5011
Menu	버섯뒤셀 & 트러플 라자냐 Mushroom Duxelles & Truffle Lasagna ₩27,000 홍합 에스카베체 Mussel Escabeche ₩24,000
Hours	17:00-24:00 월·화요일 휴무 Closed on Mondays & Tuesdays
◎	paulsdiner_

Grill
그 릴

금돼지식당
Gold Pig Restaurant

남영돈
Namyeongdon

벽제갈비 더 청담
Byeokje Galbi the Cheongdam

본앤브레드
BORN & BRED

삼원가든
Samwon Garden

세스타
Cesta

유용욱바베큐연구소
Yooyongwook BBQ Lab

한우다이닝 울릉
ULLEUNG

금돼지식당 돼지고기 바비큐 Pork BBQ
Gold Pig Restaurant

특허받은 청결연탄을 쓰는 돼지고기 연탄구이 전문점이다. 쫄깃한 식감을 위해 요크셔와 버크셔, 듀록 돼지의 교배종인 YBD 품종만을 사용한다. 갈비뼈가 붙어 있는 본삼겹과 등목살 등 흔하지 않은 돼지고기의 특수 부위도 맛볼 수 있다.

This briquette-grilled pork restaurant uses patented clean briquettes for barbecue. The restaurant uses only premium YBD pork, a hybrid of Yorkshire, Berkshire, and Durok breeds, for a chewy texture. You can enjoy a variety of special pork cuts such as bone-in pork belly and pork shoulder.

Address	서울시 중구 다산로 149 149, Dasan-ro, Jung-gu, Seoul
Tel	010-4484-8750
Menu	본삼겹 Bone-in Pork Belly ₩19,000 눈꽃목살 Grilled Pork Shoulder ₩18,000
Hours	11:30-22:00
◎	gold_pig1982

그릴 | Grill

남영돈 돼지고기 바비큐 Pork BBQ
Namyeongdon

'입에 가득 찬 고기'라는 뜻의 위트 넘치는 참숯 화로구이 전문점. 항정살, 가브리살, 삼겹살, 목살, 네 부위를 참숯에 구워 제공한다. 육즙 가득한 고기는 쫄깃한 식감이 일품이며, 조개젓갈, 가리비젓갈 등 다섯 가지 소스가 풍미를 한층 끌어올린다.

The witty name of the restaurant literally means "a mouthful of meat." The restaurant serves four types of charcoal-grilled pork cuts: pork neck, blade-end fatback, pork belly, and pork shoulder. The restaurant is popular for juicy and chewy pork dishes. It also serves five types of sauces, including salted clam and salted scallop, which upgrade the flavor of the pork.

Address	서울시 용산구 한강대로80길 17 17, Hangang-daero 80-gil, Yongsan-gu, Seoul
Tel	02-793-3598
Menu	가브리살 Blade-end Fatback ₩18,000 탱글탱글 목살 Grilled Pork Shoulder ₩20,000
Hours	16:00-22:00, 주말 Weekends 12:00-21:00
◎	namyeong_don

(NEW)
벽제갈비 더 청담 한우 비프 다이닝 Korean Beef Dining
Byeokje Galbi the Cheongdam

<벽제갈비>의 프리미엄 비프 다이닝이다. '꽃뼈생갈비'를 주문하면 30여 년 경력의 육가공 장인들이 테이블에서 직접 갈비를 해체하며 부위별 설명과 함께 구워주는 특별 서비스를 보여준다. 한우와 해산물이 매끄럽게 교차되는 한식 오마카세도 마련됐다.

Byeokje Galbi the Cheongdam is a premium beef dining restaurant by "Byeokje Galbi." If you order Grilled Bone-in Galbi, a meat processing expert with 30 years of experience cuts and cooks the beef at your table with an explanation about the different cuts. The restaurant also offers the Chef's Korean Cuisine Choice consisting of Korean beef and seafood dishes.

Address	서울시 강남구 도산대로81길 25, 1층 1F, 25, Dosan-daero 81-gil, Gangnam-gu, Seoul
Tel	02-512-9593
Menu	꽃뼈생갈비(1kg) Grilled Bone-in Galbi (1kg) ₩620,000 맡김차림 Chef's Choice ₩300,000
Hours	11:30-15:00, 17:00-22:00
◎	the_bjgalbi

그릴 | Grill

본앤브레드 한우 비프 다이닝 Korean Beef Dining
BORN & BRED

프리미엄 한우 맘김차림 열풍을 불러일으킨 근원지 중 한 곳으로 꼽힌다. 한우 장인의 경험과 역사를 바탕으로 최상 등급의 한우를 오마카세 형태로 선보인다. 정육점, 캐주얼 다이닝, 프라이빗 다이닝 등 1층부터 4층까지 다른 콘셉트로 운영된다.

BORN & BRED is known as one of the restaurants that popularized premium Korean beef omakase. The restaurant presents premium Korean beef omakase meals based on the experience and career of Korean beef experts. The four-story restaurant operates with different concepts on each floor, including butcher's shop, casual dining, and private dining.

Address	서울시 성동구 마장로 42길 1 1, Majang-ro 42-gil, Seongdong-gu, Seoul
Tel	02-2294-5005
Menu	한우 맘김차림 Korean Beef Omakase ₩350,000 샤브 맘김차림(2인) Shabu Omakase (for 2 people) ₩99,000
Hours	12:00-15:00, 18:00-22:30
◉	bornandbredkorea

삼원가든 한우 비프 다이닝 Korean Beef Dining
Samwon Garden

1976년 설립된 고급 가든형 갈빗집으로, 최근 새 단장하여 리오픈했다. 대표 메뉴인 양념갈비는 다이아몬드 모양으로 칼집을 내고, 숯불 위에 올린 황동 불판에 구워 은은한 숯 향이 특징이다. 46년 전통의 달짝지근한 비법 양념도 자꾸만 손이 가게 만드는 매력 요소.

Samwon Garden is a premium galbi restaurant opened in 1976, and was recently redecorated and reopened. Grilled Marinated Galbi is its signature dish, with shallow cuts made to the meat then charcoal-grilled for a smoky flavor. The house galbi sauce with a 46-year history captivates your taste buds.

Address	서울시 강남구 언주로 835 835, Eonju-ro, Gangnam-gu, Seoul
Tel	02-548-3030
Menu	삼원 전통 양념갈비 Samwon Traditional Grilled Marinated Galbi ₩50,000 한우 갈비(양념/생) Korean Galbi (Marinated/Fresh) ₩100,000
Hours	11:30–15:00, 17:00–22:00
	sg_dinehill

그릴 | Grill

세스타 그릴 다이닝 Grill Dining
Cesta

드라이에이징 스테이크 전문점 <휴135>의 김세경 셰프의 컨템퍼러리 그릴 다이닝이다. 숯을 활용해 재료 본연의 특성이 돋보이는 직관적인 메뉴를 선보인다. 채소부터 해산물, 육류까지 폭넓은 재료를 다루며 다채로운 요리를 구현한다.

It is a contemporary grilled dining restaurant opened by chef Kim Se-kyeong of "Hue 135", a steakhouse specializing in dry-aged steaks. The restaurant serves intuitive dishes using charcoal, emphasizing the original character of the ingredients. It uses a wide range of ingredients including vegetables, seafood, and meat for diverse dishes.

Address	서울시 용산구 한남대로20길 21-18, 1층 1F, 21-18, Hannam-daero 20-gil, Yongsan-gu, Seoul
Tel	02-793-9400
Menu	오늘의 생선 통구이 Today's Grilled Whole Fish ₩180,000 한우 본매로 Korean Beef Marrow ₩24,000
Hours	화·수요일 Tuesday & Wednesday 13:00-16:00, 17:00-23:00 목-토요일 Thursday-Saturday 13:00-16:00, 17:00-24:00 일요일 Sunday 13:00-16:00, 17:00-22:00 월요일 휴무 Closed on Mondays
	cesta.seoul

유용욱바베큐연구소 스모크드 바비큐 Smoked BBQ
Yooyongwook BBQ Lab

프라이빗한 공간에서 바비큐 코스 요리를 즐기는 원테이블 바비큐 다이닝이다. 참나무 장작에 구운 고기 요리를 중심으로 8-9가지 다양한 메뉴를 코스로 선보인다. 상호에 걸맞게 치킨버거, 타코 등의 실험적인 창작 메뉴를 끊임없이 개발한다.

It is a one-table barbecue dining restaurant where you can enjoy a barbecue course meal in a private space. The restaurant offers eight to nine dishes in a course, serving meat dishes grilled on oak firewood. Befitting the name of the restaurant, it continuously develops experimental dishes such as Chicken Burger and Taco.

Address	서울시 용산구 한강대로84길 5-7, 남영아케이드(안쪽 가게) Namyeong Arcade (inside the building), 5-7, Hangang-daero 84-gil, Yongsan-gu, Seoul
Tel	010-4275-1177
Menu	코스 Course ₩135,000
Hours	화-토요일 Tuesday-Saturday 11:00-21:30 일·월요일 휴무 Closed on Sundays & Mondays
◎	yooyongwook

그릴 | Grill

한우다이닝 울릉 한우 비프 다이닝 Korean Beef Dining
ULLEUNG

<서관면옥> 김인복 셰프가 울릉도를 테마로 삼아 로컬 다이닝을 제안한다. 약초를 먹고 자란 약소와 칡소, 최상급 1++ 한우로 구성된 구이류가 인상적. 울릉도에서 자생하는 고유의 식재료를 활용한 골동면, 솥밥 등 울릉도식 식사 메뉴도 인기다.

Chef Kim In-bok of "Seogwan Myeonok" presents local dining under the theme of Ulleungdo Island. Its signature dishes are grilled premium 1++ Korean beef dishes consisting of Ulleungdo prime beef and brindle hanwoo beef from cattle fed with medicinal herbs. Ulleungdo Island-style dishes such as goldongmyeon noodles and hot stone pot rice made with regional ingredients from Ulleungdo Island are popular as well.

Address	서울시 서초구 서운로 135 135, Seoun-ro, Seocho-gu, Seoul
Tel	02-581-2235
Menu	울릉 코스 Ulleung Course ₩200,000 (주말 런치 한정 Weekend Lunch ₩150,000) 울릉칡소 모둠구이(2인 기준) Ulleung Assorted Brindle Hanwoo Beef Barbecue (for 2 people) ₩200,000
Hours	11:00-15:00, 17:30-21:30
	dining_ulleung

Plant-Based

채식

로컬릿
local EAT

마지
Maji

발우공양
Balwoo Gongyang

베이스 이즈 나이스
base is nice

베제투스
Vegetus

산촌
Sanchon

쿤
Qyun

포리스트키친
Forest Kitchen

플랜트
PLANT

로컬릿 유러피언 European
local EAT

팜투테이블을 실천하는 남정석 셰프의 채식 기반 다이닝. 농부 시장이나 소규모 농장 등에서 수급한 로컬 식재료를 활용해 건강하면서도 맛있는 유러피언 요리를 선보인다. 백태콩으로 만든 후무스와 채소를 차곡차곡 쌓은 채소 테린이 시그니처 메뉴다.

It is a vegetarian-based restaurant by chef Nam Jeong-seok, who applies farm-to-table practices. The restaurant procures local ingredients from farmers' markets or small farms to serve healthy and delicious European dishes. Its signature dishes are Hummus made with white soybean and Vegetable Terrine made with layers of vegetables.

Address	서울시 성동구 한림말길 33, 2층 2F, 33, Hallimmal-gil, Seongdong-gu, Seoul
Tel	02-2282-1124
Menu	채소 테린 Vegetable Terrine ₩16,000 시금치 뇨끼 Spinach Gnocchi ₩19,000
Hours	11:00-15:00, 17:00-21:00, 주말 Weekends 11:00-21:00
	the_local_eater

채식 | Plant-Based

마지 사찰 음식 Korean Temple Dining
Maji

사찰 음식을 바탕으로 한 채식 요리 전문점이다. 오신채를 쓰지 않고, 직접 담근 장과 무농약 채소를 활용한 자연 그대로의 맛을 식탁에 올린다. 배냉면, 호두만두 등 개성 있는 메뉴도 눈에 띈다. 대부분의 재료는 10년 이상 거래한 농가나 사찰에서 받는다.

A vegetarian restaurant specializing in Buddhist temple dishes. The restaurant presents the true flavors of nature, using handmade sauces and pesticide-free vegetables, excluding the five forbidden pungent herbs. It also serves some unique dishes such as Cold Buckwheat Noodles with Pear and Walnut Mandu. It procures most of the ingredients from farms and temples with whom it has been doing business for over 10 years.

Address	서울시 종로구 자하문로5길 19 19, Jahamun-ro 5-gil, Jongno-gu, Seoul
Tel	02-536-5228
Menu	고급 코스 Premium Course ₩40,000-60,000 런치·디너 세트 Lunch/Dinner Sets ₩21,000
Hours	11:30-15:00, 17:00-21:00 화요일 휴무 Closed on Tuesdays
Ⓦ	www.templefood.com

발우공양 사찰 음식 Korean Temple Dining
Balwoo Gongyang

대한불교 조계종에서 직접 운영하고 있는 사찰 음식 전문 레스토랑. 유기농 채소를 주요 식재료로 사용하며, 직접 담근 전통 장과 최소한의 양념만을 더해 속이 편안한 코스 요리를 내놓는다. 별실로 된 아늑한 공간에서 수행 음식 문화를 음미할 수 있다.

A restaurant specializing in temple dishes, run by the Jogye Order of Korean Buddhism. You can enjoy a temple food course meal consisting of easily digestible dishes made with mainly organic vegetables, seasoned with handmade traditional sauces and minimal seasonings. You can experience the food culture of spiritual cultivation in a cozy private room.

Address	서울시 종로구 우정국로 56, 5층 5F, 56, Ujeongguk-ro, Jongno-gu, Seoul
Tel	010-2956-3493, 02-733-2081
Menu	원식 코스 메뉴 Won Course ₩45,000 마음식 코스 메뉴 Maeum Course ₩65,000
Hours	11:30-13:20(런치 1부) (Lunch 1), 13:30-14:50(런치 2부) (Lunch 2), 18:00-21:30 일요일 휴무 Closed on Sundays
〇	balwoogongyang_official

채식 | Plant-Based

베이스 이즈 나이스 모던 한식 Modern Korean
base is nice

다양한 방식으로 채소 본연의 맛과 향을 살린 채소 중심의 다이닝이다. 삶고 데치는 한식 조리법에서 벗어나, 말리거나 굽거나 훈연하는 등 다양한 조리법을 접목한 것이 특징. 튀긴 청무와 구운 옥수수 등 각종 채소를 밥 위에 얹은 채소밥은 익숙하면서도 색다르다.

A vegetarian-based restaurant that presents the original flavors and aromas of vegetables in diverse ways. The restaurant uses a variety of techniques such as drying, grilling, and smoking instead of adhering to traditional Korean methods such as boiling and parboiling. Vegetable rice made with steamed rice and topped with various vegetables such as deep-fried radish and baked corn is familiar yet unique.

Address 서울시 마포구 도화2길 20
20, Dohwa 2-gil, Mapo-gu, Seoul
Tel 010-9617-6724
Menu 바삭 청무와 옥수수 밥 Crunchy Radish and Corn Rice ₩20,000
무화과를 올린 발효버터 햇우엉구이 밥
Fresh Grilled Burdock Root Rice with Fermented Butter and Fig ₩20,000
Hours 11:30-15:00
월요일 휴무 Closed on Mondays

baseisnice_seoul

베제투스 유러피언 European
Vegetus

해방촌에 위치한 식물성 요리 전문점이다. 대표 메뉴인 베제투스버거는 시중의 햄버거와 달리 렌틸콩과 양파, 버섯으로 만든 패티를 사용해 고소한 맛과 부드러운 식감을 살렸다. 바질과 마늘을 혼합한 페스토, 스리라차 마요네즈 등의 소스는 감칠맛을 더하는 요소.

A vegetarian restaurant located in Haebangchon. The signature dish, Vegetus Burger, features a savory flavor and soft texture for its patty made with lentils, onions, and mushrooms. Its special sauces such as basil and garlic-mixed pesto and sriracha mayo upgrade the taste of the dishes.

Address	서울시 용산구 신흥로 59 59, Sinheung-ro, Yongsan-gu, Seoul
Tel	070-8824-5959
Menu	라자냐 Lasagna ₩17,000 베제투스버거 Vegetus Burger ₩14,000
Hours	평일 Weekdays 12:00-15:00, 17:00-21:30, 주말 Weekends 12:00-21:30
◎	vegetuskr

채식 | Plant-Based

산촌 사찰 음식 Korean Temple Dining
Sanchon

인사동 부근의 사찰 음식 전문점으로, 산속에서 자라는 채소와 나물을 주재료로 한다. 야생초를 활용한 한식 반상 차림을 비롯해 다양한 계절 반찬을 맛볼 수 있다. 한옥 구조의 공간 곳곳에 놓인 식물과 사찰 소품들로 고즈넉한 분위기를 자아낸다.

A Buddhist temple food restaurant located in Insa-dong. The restaurant uses mainly wild vegetables and edible greens. It serves Korean set menus made with wild vegetables and other various seasonal side dishes. Plants and Buddhist temple items placed in this hanok restaurant create a peaceful atmosphere.

Address 서울시 종로구 인사동길 30-13
30-13, Insadong-gil, Jongno-gu, Seoul
Tel 02-735-0312
Menu 산촌 정식(점심) Sanchon Set Menu (Lunch) ₩29,000
산촌 정식(저녁) Sanchon Set Menu (Dinner) ₩29,000
Hours 12:00-20:30
Ⓦ www.sanchon.com

큔 그로서리 카페 Grocery Café
Qyun

그로서리와 카페로 운영되는 서촌의 발효 식품 음식점. 다양한 발효 기법을 응용한 채소 중심의 요리와 건강 음료를 즐길 수 있다. 공간 한편의 '큔상점'에서는 삼발 토마토소스, 알알이 머스터드 피클, 금귤 발효 소금 등의 발효 조미료와 소스를 판매하고 있다.

A fermented food restaurant in Seochon, which is both a grocery store and café. You can enjoy healthy beverages and vegetable dishes made with a variety of fermentation techniques. Qyun Grocery Store, located in the corner of the restaurant, sells fermented seasonings and sauces such as sambal tomato sauce, mustard pickles, and fermented kumquat salt.

Address 서울시 종로구 자하문로26길 17-2, 1층
1F, 17-2, Jahamun-ro 26-gil, Jongno-gu, Seoul
Tel 010-3707-3711
Menu 구운 채소와 비건발효버터 커리
Grilled Vegetables with Fermented Vegan Butter Curry ₩16,000
템페와 삼발토마토소스 핫 샌드위치
Tempeh Sambal Tomato Sauce Hot Sandwich ₩9,000
Hours 11:00-16:00
월·화요일 휴무 Closed on Mondays & Tuesdays

grocery_cafe_qyun

채식 | Plant-Based

포리스트키친 이노베이티브 Innovative
Forest Kitchen

식탁 위의 지속가능성을 추구하는 프리미엄 비건 다이닝. 뉴욕 미쉐린 레스토랑 출신의 김태형 총괄 셰프가 제철 재료와 대체육을 활용해 코스 요리를 선보인다. 주된 식재료인 채소류는 파주의 유기농 직영 농장에서 매일 아침 배달 받는다.

A premium vegan restaurant pursuing food sustainability. Head chef Kim Tae-hyeong, who used to work for a Michelin restaurant in New York, presents course meals made with seasonal ingredients and plant-based meat. Its main ingredients of vegetables are delivered directly every morning from an organic farm in Paju.

Address	서울시 송파구 올림픽로 300, 롯데월드몰 6층
	6F, Lotte World Mall, 300, Olympic-ro, Songpa-gu, Seoul
Tel	02-3213-4626
Menu	런치 코스 Lunch Course ₩55,000
	디너 코스 Dinner Course ₩77,000
Hours	11:00-15:00, 17:00-22:00
	forestkitchen.official

플랜트 다이닝 카페 Dining Café
PLANT

이름처럼 푸릇푸릇한 식물로 꾸며진 싱그러운 분위기의 비건 다이닝 카페다.
병아리콩으로 만든 후무스와 단호박을 곁들인 샐러드가 대표 메뉴로 각광받고 있다.
버거나 파스타 등 친숙한 식사 메뉴와 함께 비건 맥주, 와인이 구비되어 있다.

A vegan restaurant and café decorated with plants just like its name. The restaurant is popular for its signature dish, a salad served with sweet pumpkin and hummus made with chick peas. It serves vegan beer and wine as well as familiar dishes such as burgers and pasta.

Address	서울시 용산구 보광로 117, 2층 2F, 117, Bogwang-ro, Yongsan-gu, Seoul
Tel	02-749-1981
Menu	후무스 단호박 샐러드 Hummus Sweet Pumpkin Salad ₩14,500 렌틸 베지볼 Lentil Veggie Bowl ₩13,000
Hours	11:00-22:00
📷	plantcafeseoul

채식 | Plant-Based

Café & Dessert

카페 & 디저트

강정이넘치는집
Gangjeong house

김씨부인
Kimssibooin

담장옆에국화꽃 인사동점
CCOT (Insa-dong Branch)

메종엠오
Maison M.O

삐아프
Piaf

소나
SONA

아뜰리에퐁드
Atelier POND

재인
JAEIN

제이엘디저트바
JL DESSERT BAR

프릳츠 컴퍼니 도화점
FRITZ COFFEE

합 원서점
HAAP

강정이넘치는집 한식 디저트 Korean Dessert
Gangjeong house

형제가 의기투합해 전국 각지에서 얻은 재료로 만든 전통 병과를 선보인다. 강정을 에너지 바로 개발하는 등 과거와 현재의 조화를 추구한다. 깨말이강정은 얇게 편 강정 위에 피스타치오와 무화과, 피칸 등을 올린 시그너처 메뉴.

The brothers make traditional rice cakes and confections using ingredients from all over the country. They pursue the harmony of the past and present, developing new dessert dishes such as a sweet rice puff energy bar. The signature item, the sweet rice and sesame puff, is a thin sweet rice puff topped with pistachios, fig, and pecan.

Address	서울시 강남구 학동로 435, 1층
	1F, 435, Hakdong-ro, Gangnam-gu, Seoul
Tel	02-2201-0447
Menu	12구 한식디저트 견과류 깨말이 세트
	Korean Nut & Sesame Dessert Set (12 pieces) ₩60,000
	한식디저트 개성약과 Korean Dessert Gaeseong Honey Cookie ₩9,000
Hours	07:00-22:00
	gj_house

카페 & 디저트 | Café & Dessert

김씨부인 한식 디저트 Korean Dessert
Kimssibooin

조선시대 양반가의 반상 문화에 착안해 한식 디저트를 상차림 형태로 내어주는 전통 카페다. 떡, 단자, 정과 같은 달달한 병과와 지역 전통차를 맛뿐만이 아니라 모양의 어울림까지 고려해 차려낸다. 가을에는 사과정과, 겨울에는 딸기단자 등 제철 재료를 사용한다.

This traditional Korean dessert café serves Korean desserts on a small dining table, inspired by the private table culture of noble houses in the Joseon Dynasty. You can enjoy a platter of sweet rice cakes, rice cake balls, and candied desserts with a cup of traditional local tea, which creates harmony both in flavor and presentation. It serves candied apples in autumn and strawberry rice cake balls in the summer using seasonal ingredients.

Address 서울시 서초구 사평대로26길 26-6, 2층
2F, 26-6, Sapyeong-daero 26-gil, Seocho-gu, Seoul
Tel 02-532-5327
Menu 소반차림세트(1인 특, 티 포함) Soban Set (For 1 person, tea included) ₩25,000-33,000
개성주악 Gaeseong Juak ₩4,000
Hours 13:00-19:00
일요일 휴무 Closed on Sundays

kimssibooin_korean_dessert

담장옆에 국화꽃 인사동점 한식 디저트 Korean Dessert
CCOT (Insa-dong Branch)

전통에 현대적 요소를 더한 병과를 다양한 음료와 즐길 수 있는 전통 병과 카페다. 전국떡명장대회에서 제6대 떡 명장으로 선정된 오숙경 대표가 레시피를 총괄한다. 팥빙수 위에 팥 아이스크림을 얹은 팥바팥빙수 등 감각적인 메뉴로 젊은 층에게 인기다.

You can enjoy traditional rice cakes and confections augmented with a modern touch with a variety of beverages at this café. It is run by CEO Oh Suk-kyeong, who was selected as the sixth master of rice cakes at the National Rice Cake Master Contest. Its trendy desserts, such as Shaved Ice with Red Beans topped with red bean ice cream, are especially popular with younger generations.

Address	서울시 종로구 인사동길 49, 2층 2F, 49, Insadong-gil, Jongno-gu, Seoul
Tel	02-6954-2979
Menu	팥바팥빙수 Shaved Ice with Red Beans ₩12,900 팥죽(고운단팥죽, 통단팥죽, 무가당통팥죽) Red Bean Porridge (Smooth Red Bean Porridge/Whole Red Bean Porridge/Non-sugar Whole Red Bean Porridge) ₩8,800
Hours	11:00-21:00
◉	ccot_insa

카페 & 디저트 | Café & Dessert

메종엠오 베이커리 Bakery
Maison M.O

<피에르 에르메> 도쿄지점에서 부부의 연을 맺은 오오츠카 테츠야, 이민선 파티시에의 파티스리다. 클래식한 레시피를 이곳만의 감성으로 풀어낸 디저트를 매일 한정 수량 판매한다. 마들렌, 초코파이 등 익숙한 메뉴에서 새로운 맛을 느낄 수 있다.

A pâtisserie run by a married pâtissier couple, Tetsuya Otsuka and Lee Min-sun, who met at "Pierre Hermé Tokyo." The pâtisserie offers limited amounts of classic desserts made with its own recipes. You will have a new experience from familiar desserts such as madeleines and chocolate pie.

Address	서울시 서초구 방배로 26길 22, 1층 1F, 22, Bangbae-ro 26-gil, Seocho-gu, Seoul
Tel	070-4239-3335
Menu	기본 마들렌 Basic Madeleine ₩3,000 휘낭시에 Financier ₩3,000
Hours	목-일요일 Thursday-Sunday 11:30-20:00 월-수요일 휴무 Closed on Mondays through Wednesdays
	maison_m.o

삐아프 초콜릿 Chocolate
Piaf

고은수 셰프가 운영하는 프렌치 수제 초콜릿 숍이다. 고급 프랑스산 커버처, 게랑드 천일염, AOP 버터 등 프리미엄 재료만을 사용한 명품 초콜릿들이 보석처럼 빛난다. 서울에서 가장 클래식한 초콜릿 봉봉을 만날 수 있는 곳이다.

A French handmade chocolate shop run by chef Ko Eun-soo. The chocolate shop offers jewel-like chocolates made only with premium ingredients such as premium French couverture, Guérande sun-dried salt, and AOP butter. This is the place where you can find the most classic chocolate bonbon in Seoul.

Address	서울시 강남구 논현로175길 109, 1층 1F, 109, Nonhyeon-ro 175-gil, Gangnam-gu, Seoul
Tel	02-545-0317
Menu	천일염 프랄리네 Sun-dried Salt Praline ₩2,800 유자 Citrus ₩2,800
Hours	12:30-19:30 일요일 휴무 Closed on Sundays
	piaf_artisan_chocolatier

카페 & 디저트 | Café & Dessert

소나 디저트 Dessert
SONA

주문 즉시 만들어 선보이는 성현아 파티시에의 코스 디저트 숍이다. 제철 재료로 만드는 3코스 디저트와 식용 꽃을 올려 장식미를 더한 샴페인 슈가볼이 대표 메뉴다. 코스 마지막에는 쁘띠푸 8종 중 입맛에 따라 골라 즐길 수 있다.

Pâtissier Seong Hyeon-ah's dessert course shop, offering desserts prepared to order. The 3-course Desserts and Drink Set made with seasonal ingredients and the Champagne Sugar Ball decorated with edible flowers are its signature dishes. You can enjoy one of the eight types of petit fours at the end of the course.

Address 서울시 강남구 강남대로162길 40, 2층
2F, 40, Gangnam-daero 162-gil, Gangnam-gu, Seoul
Tel 02-515-3246
Menu 3코스 디저트와 음료세트 3-course Desserts and Drink Set ₩28,000
샴페인 슈가볼 Champagne Sugar Ball ₩18,000
Hours 12:30-22:00
화요일 휴무 Closed on Tuesdays

sona_seoul

아뜰리에퐁드 디저트 Dessert
Atelier POND

김유정 셰프가 선보이는 하이엔드 디저트 숍이다. 진하고 깊은 맛의 캐러멜 바가 인기 메뉴. 일러스트가 그려진 페이퍼와 메이플 원목 상자가 그 맛의 기품을 더한다. 100% 사전 예약제로 매일 한정 수량만 판매한다.

A high-end dessert shop that prepares desserts made by chef Kim Yu-jeong. Its signature dessert is a Caramel Bar with deep and rich flavor. A maple wood box and illustrated paper upgrade the allure of the desserts. Desserts are sold in limited amounts daily, by reservation only.

Address 서울시 용산구 한남대로27길 19
             19, Hannam-daero 27-gil, Yongsan-gu, Seoul
Tel   010-7764-7663
Menu   캐러멜 바 Caramel Bar ₩82,000
             쿠키 박스 Cookie Box ₩88,000
Hours   12:00-17:00
             일·월요일 휴무 Closed on Sundays & Mondays

atelier.pond

카페 & 디저트 | Café & Dessert

NEW

재인 디저트 Dessert
JAEIN

제철 과일을 활용해 디저트의 맛을 최상으로 느낄 수 있는 파티스리다. 이재인 셰프가 한국의 식재료를 유러피언 디저트 메뉴에 접목하여 절묘하게 풀어낸다. 쑥 마들렌, 된장 브라우니 등의 메뉴와 나무, 검은숲 등 독특한 모양의 메뉴를 즐길 수 있다.

A pâtisserie serving premium desserts made with seasonal fruits. Chef Lee Jae-in uses Korean ingredients for European dessert recipes. You can enjoy Mugwort Madeleine and Soybean Paste Brownie as well as some unique shaped desserts such as Trees and Black Forest.

Address	서울시 용산구 이태원로54길 48, 2층
	2F, 48, Itaewon-ro 54-gil, Yongsan-gu, Seoul
Tel	02-797-2454
Menu	나무 Trees ₩7,800
	검은숲 Black Forest ₩35,000
Hours	13:00-19:00
	수·목요일 휴무 Closed on Wednesdays & Thursdays
◎	patisserie.jaein

제이엘디저트바 디저트 Dessert
JL DESSERT BAR

디저트를 독립된 하나의 요리처럼 선보이는 디저트 바다. 이탈리언 요리사 경력의 저스틴 리 셰프가 그만의 감각으로 풀어낸 디저트 메뉴를 맛볼 수 있다. 특히 디저트를 두루 경험할 수 있는 테이스팅 코스와 셰프 추천 주류의 마리아주가 각별하다.

A dessert bar where you can taste desserts as à la carte cuisine. Chef Justin Lee, a chef experienced in Italian cuisine, makes desserts in his unique fashion. You can try the Tasting Course to enjoy the different types of desserts and its pairing with liquors recommended by the chef is outstanding.

Address	서울시 용산구 이태원로55가길 38, 2층
	2F, 38, Itaewon-ro 55ga-gil, Yongsan-gu, Seoul
Tel	02-543-6140
Menu	플레이트 디저트 Plate Dessert ₩12,000-17,000
	디저트 테이스팅 메뉴 Dessert Tasting Course ₩55,000
Hours	월-금요일 Monday-Friday 13:00-17:00, 18:00-22:00
	토요일 Saturday 13:00-23:00, 일요일 Sunday 13:00-21:00
	jldessertbar

카페 & 디저트 | Café & Dessert

프릳츠 컴퍼니 도화점 카페 Café
FRITZ COFFEE

오래된 양옥집을 개조한 뉴트로 콘셉트의 이른바 '코리안 빈티지' 카페다. 생원두를 가열 시간을 줄여 로스팅한 원두로 이곳만의 개성파 커피를 선보인다. 블루베리 파이, 커피번 등 매일 아침 구워내는 베이커리류도 다채롭다.

A Korean vintage café with the concept of newtro, housed in a renovated old Western-style house. By roasting fresh coffee beans for a shorter period of time, the café presents a unique flavor of coffee. It also offers a variety of bakery products such as blueberry pie and coffee bun.

Address	서울시 마포구 새창로2길 17 17, Saechang-ro 2-gil, Mapo-gu, Seoul
Tel	02-3275-2045
Menu	아메리카노 Americano ₩4,600 카페라떼 Caffè Latte ₩5,000
Hours	평일 Weekdays 08:00-23:00, 주말 Weekends 10:00-23:00
◎	fritzcoffeecompany

합 원서점 한식 디저트 Korean Dessert
HAAP

한식 병과의 명맥을 이어가는 신용일 셰프의 한식 디저트 카페다. 전통 레시피에 모던한 디자인을 더해 세련된 병과를 만날 수 있다. 달콤쌉쌀한 생강 향 주악, 쫄깃한 떡살이 일품인 바람떡 등의 메뉴를 만날 수 있으며, 디저트 코스도 준비됐다.

A Korean dessert café run by chef Shin Yong-il, who continues the legacy of Korean traditional rice cakes and confections. The café serves sophisticated rice cakes and confections based on traditional recipes and modern design. Bitter-sweet ginger-flavored juak and half-moon-shaped chewy rice cakes captivate your taste buds. You can also enjoy a dessert course.

Address 서울시 종로구 율곡로 83, 신관 2층
2F, New Building, 83, Yulgok-ro, Jongno-gu, Seoul
Tel 010-5027-8190
Menu 구구상자 선물세트(병과 9가지+광목보자기 포장) Gugu Gift Box
(9 types of rice cakes & confections + cotton wrapping cloth packaging) ₩20,000
배숙음료 Baesuk Beverage ₩6,000
Hours 12:00-18:00
월·화요일 휴무 Closed on Mondays & Tuesdays

haap2010

카페 & 디저트 | Café & Dessert

Bar&Pub
바 & 펍

까사델비노 청담점
Casa del Vino

르챔버
Le Chamber

뮤땅
MUTIN

바 뽐
Bar Pomme

바 참
BAR CHAM

바 피크닉
Bar piknic

백곰막걸리
Whitebear Makgeolli Bar

뱅글
Vingle

서울집시
Seoulgypsy

오네뜨장
Honnêtes Gens

제스트
ZEST

찰스 H.
CHARLES H.

파인앤코
Pine & Co

까사델비노 청담점 와인 바 Wine Bar
Casa del Vino

2002년 오픈 후 국내 와인 신에 한 획을 그은 와인 바다. 7백여 종의 리스트와 소믈리에의 전문적인 서비스로 20년의 견고한 역사를 잇고 있다. 메뉴 또한 수준급인데, 달랑무 김치피클을 곁들여 먹는 알리오올리오가 스테디셀러다.

An epoch-making wine bar in Korea since its opening in 2002. It has been continuing its 20-year-old history with its sommeliers' professional service and a wine list containing around 700 wines. The wine bar is also renowned for its quality dishes. In particular, Spaghetti Aglio e Olio served with kimchi pickles is a steady seller.

Address	서울시 강남구 선릉로162길 43, 1층 1F, 43, Seolleung-ro 162-gil, Gangnam-gu, Seoul
Tel	02-542-8003
Menu	백합조개 봉골레파스타 Vongole Pasta ₩32,000 오리가슴살 스테이크 Duck Breast Streak ₩38,000
Hours	18:00-02:00 명절 휴무 Closed on Lunar New Year's Day and Chuseok
◉	casadelvino2002

바 & 펍 | Bar & Pub

르챔버 칵테일 바 Cocktail Bar
Le Chamber

2014년 오픈 후 국내 바 신에서 정상의 위치를 유지하고 있는 바다. 글로벌 무대에서 실력을 인정받은 임재진·엄도환 오너 바텐더가 직접 엄선한 위스키 라인업을 즐길 수 있다. 이곳만의 스타일로 재해석한 모스코 뮬인 '챔버 뮬'이 단연 스테디셀러.

Le Chamber has remained No. 1 in Korea since its opening in 2014. You can enjoy a whiskey lineup carefully selected by owner bartenders Lim Jae-jin and Uhm Do-hwan, who are globally well known. Chamber Mule, a Moscow mule reinterpreted in the bar's own style, is a steady seller.

Address 서울시 강남구 도산대로55길 42
42, Dosan-daero 55-gil, Gangnam-gu, Seoul
Tel 02-6337-2014
Menu 챔버스토리 Chamber Story ₩27,000
래핑부다 Laughing Buddha ₩27,000
Hours 월-목요일 Monday-Thursday 19:00-03:00
금·토요일 Friday & Saturday 19:00-04:00
일요일 Sunday 19:00-02:00

le_chamber

뮤땅 와인 바 Wine Bar
MUTIN

홍강석 셰프의 컨템퍼러리 와인 바. 비스트로노미한 요리와 함께 내추럴 와인을 즐길 수 있다. 드라이에이징 생선 요리와 스테이크, 농어 선어회에 아삭한 노각과 새콤달콤한 패션프루츠를 얹은 농어 디시 등 프렌치 베이스의 개성 있는 메뉴가 가득하다.

A contemporary wine bar run by chef Hong Gang-seok. You can enjoy bistronomy-style dishes with natural wines. The wine bar serves French cuisine-based unique dishes such as dry-aged fish and steak and sliced aged raw sea bass served with crunch yellow cucumber and sweet-and-sour passion fruit.

Address	서울시 용산구 대사관로12길 4-2, 2층 2F, 4-2, Daesagwan-ro 12-gil, Yongsan-gu, Seoul
Tel	070-7776-3052
Menu	전복, 폴렌타, 스페츨 Abalone, Polenta, and Spätzle ₩26,000 오리가슴살, 사우어도우퓨레, 무화과 Duck Breast, Sourdough Puree, and Fig ₩32,000
Hours	18:00-24:00, 토요일 Saturday 16:00-24:00 일·월요일 휴무 Closed on Sundays & Mondays
	mutin_bar

바 & 펍 | Bar & Pub

바 쁨 칵테일 바 Cocktail Bar
Bar Pomme

서촌의 <바 참> 임병진 바텐더가 운영하는 세컨드 바다. 업장명은 프랑스어로 '사과'를 뜻하는데, 사과를 비롯한 과일과 채소를 참신하게 해석한 '팜 칵테일'을 맛볼 수 있다. 당근 칵테일 '24캐럿' 등 작명 센스도 남다르다.

A second bar by bartender Lim Byeong-jin of "Bar Cham" in Seochon. The name of the bar means "apple" in French. The bar serves "farm cocktails" made with fruits and vegetables including apples. It is also well known for witty cocktail names such as 24 Carrot(Carat), referring to the carrot cocktail.

Address	서울시 종로구 자하문로9길 15, 1층 1F, 15, Jahamun-ro 9-gil, Jongno-gu, Seoul
Tel	02-725-4750
Menu	노르망디뮬 Normandy Mule ₩19,000 팜리조트 Palm Resort ₩20,000
Hours	15:00-24:00 월요일 휴무 Closed on Mondays
◎	pomme_bar

바 참
칵테일 바 Cocktail Bar
BAR CHAM

제철 식재료와 우리 술로 창의적인 칵테일을 선보이는 서촌의 한옥 바다. 여름에는 수박을 활용한 '함안 펀치'를 준비하는가 하면, 차이나타운으로 유명한 인천의 도시명을 딴 춘장 칵테일이 독특하다. 업장명은 인테리어 주요 자재인 참나무에서 따왔다.

A hanok bar in Seochon, offering creative cocktails made with seasonal ingredients and traditional Korean liquors. In the summer, the bar serves Haman Punch made with watermelon. One of its unique cocktails is the chunjang cocktail named after Incheon, the city popular of its China Town. The bar is named after oak (cham namu in Korean), the main material of its interior design.

Address	서울시 종로구 자하문로7길 34 34, Jahamun-ro 7-gil, Jongno-gu, Seoul
Tel	02-6402-4750
Menu	함안펀치 Haman Punch ₩20,000 송편 Half-moon Rice Cake ₩21,000
Hours	18:00-01:00 화요일 휴무 Closed on Tuesdays
◎	bar.cham

바 & 펍 | Bar & Pub

바 피크닉 와인 바 Wine Bar
Bar piknic

<제로컴플렉스>에서 운영하는 캐주얼 와인 바다. 이성훈 셰프가 제철 재료로 조리한 타파스 메뉴와 윤혜진 소믈리에가 엄선한 내추럴 와인의 페어링을 즐길 수 있다. 로메스코 소스를 올린 구운 대파와 알감자, 그리고 쫀득한 치즈 츄러스가 대표 메뉴.

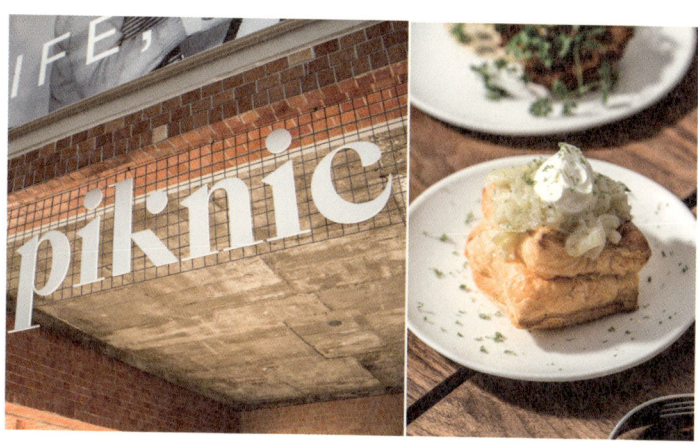

A casual wine bar run by "Zero Complex." You can enjoy the pairing of tapas made with seasonal ingredients by chef Lee Seong-hun and some natural wines selected by sommelier Yoon Hye-jin. Grilled green onions and baby potatoes with romesco sauce and chewy cheese churros are its signature dishes.

Address 서울시 중구 퇴계로6가길 30
  30, Toegye-ro 6ga-gil, Jung-gu, Seoul
Tel 02-3789-0876
Menu 치즈 츄러스 Cheese Churros ₩12,000
  이베리코 꽈리고추 Ibérico Green Chili Peppers ₩27,000
Hours 17:00-23:30
  월·화요일 휴무 Closed on Mondays & Tuesdays

barpiknic

백곰막걸리 전통주점 Traditional Liquor Bar
Whitebear Makgeolli Bar

3백50여 종 이상의 우리 술과 한식이 있는 전통 주점이다. 탁주와 청주는 물론 약주와 소주까지 빼곡한 주류 리스트가 인상적인데, 이승훈 대표가 전국 양조장을 다니며 모은 결실이다. 벌교 피꼬막무침, 태안 간재미찜 등 지역 특산물로 만든 안주 메뉴도 인상적이다.

A traditional Korean liquor bar serving Korean dishes and over 350 kinds of Korean liquor. The impressive traditional liquor list includes medicinal herb liquor and soju as well as takju (unrefined rice wine) and cheongju (refined rice wine). This is the result of the efforts of CEO Lee Seung-hoon, who visited countless breweries all over the country. The bar also serves some unique snacks made with local specialties, including Beolgyo Seasoned Ark Clams and Taean Braised Red Stingray.

Address	서울시 강남구 압구정로48길 39 39, Apgujeong-ro 48-gil, Gangnam-gu, Seoul
Tel	010-6822-7644
Menu	오징어김치전 Squid and Kimchi Pancake ₩24,000 왕째복 맑은탕 Clam Soup ₩36,000
Hours	월-목요일 Monday-Thursday 17:30-23:30 금요일 Friday 17:30-01:30, 토요일 Saturday 16:00-01:30 일요일 휴무 Closed on Sundays
	whitebear_mak

바 & 펍 | Bar & Pub

(NEW)
뱅글 와인 바 Wine Bar
Vingle

내추럴 와인과 맛깔스럽고 캐주얼한 메뉴를 즐길 수 있는 성수동 와인 바다. <밍글스>의 강민구 셰프가 내추럴 와인 전문 수입사 뱅브로와 합작해 오픈했다. 바질 파스타나 프렌치 토스트 등 유러피언 메뉴에 간장, 고추장, 된장 등 한식 터치를 가미한 메뉴가 특징이다.

A wine bar in Seongsu-dong, serving natural wines and delicious casual dishes. Chef Kang Min-goo of "Mingles" opened the wine bar in collaboration with the natural wine importing company "Vinbro." It features European dishes augmented with a Korean touch. For example, Western dishes such as Basil Pasta and French Toast are augmented with traditional Korean sauces like soy sauce, red chili paste, and soybean paste.

Address	서울시 성동구 연무장18길 16
	16, Yeonmujang 18-gil, Seongdong-gu, Seoul
Tel	02-465-7306
Menu	바질 파스타와 제철 나물 Basil Pasta & Seasonal Salad ₩18,000
	프렌치 토스트와 잠봉 French Toast & Jambon ₩13,000
Hours	12:00–15:00, 16:00–24:00
◉	vingle_seongsu

서울집시 브루어리 & 펍 Brewery & Pub
Seoulgypsy

NEW

이현오 대표의 진두지휘 아래 개발된 실험적인 맥주가 매력인 캐주얼 펍이다. 한국의 제철 재료를 활용해 계절마다 가장 맛있는 맥주 페어링을 만날 수 있다. 경남 사천의 토종 쌀을 베이스로 고수 씨앗과 오렌지 껍질을 넣은 밀맥주 서울몽이 시그너처 비어.

A casual pub serving experimental beers developed under the leadership of CEO Lee Hyeon-oh. You can enjoy the most delicious pairing of beer made with Korean seasonal ingredients. The signature beer is Seoul Mong, wheat beer made with coriander seeds, orange zest, and rice cultivated in Sacheon, Gyeongnam.

Address	서울시 종로구 서순라길 107 107, Seosulla-gil, Jongno-gu, Seoul
Tel	02-743-1212
Menu	서울몽 Seoul Mong ₩7,900 미션! 헬레스 Mission! Helles ₩7,900
Hours	16:00-23:00 월요일 휴무 Closed on Mondays
⃝	seoulgypsy

바 & 펍 | Bar & Pub

오네뜨 장 와인 바 Wine Bar
Honnêtes Gens

<비스트로 드 욘트빌>의 네오 파리지앵 와인 바다. 랍스터 누들 등 프렌치 요리에 동남아풍 요리를 결합한 메뉴를 선보인다. 6시부터는 테이스팅 코스, 9시부터는 단품 메뉴 위주로 운영되며, 코스를 주문하면 와인, 전통주, 맥주 등 다양한 페어링 주류를 추천한다.

A neo-Parisien wine bar by "Bistrot de Yountville." The wine bar presents fusion French dishes combined with Southeast Asian dishes such as Lobster Noodles. It mainly serves tasting courses from 6 p.m. and à la carte from 9 p.m. When you order a course meal, you will get a recommendation for liquor pairing such as wine, traditional liquor, and beer.

Address	서울시 강남구 선릉로158길 13-7, 지하 1층 B1, 13-7, Seolleung-ro 158-gil, Gangnam-gu, Seoul
Tel	02-545-1550
Menu	테이스팅 코스 Tasting Course ₩140,000 장어 반미(알라 카르트) Eel banh mi (À La Carte) ₩21,000
Hours	17:30-24:00 일·월요일 휴무 Closed on Sundays & Mondays
	honnetes_gens

제스트 칵테일 바 Cocktail Bar
ZEST

토닉워터를 직접 제조해 용기 배출을 줄이고, 과일 껍질을 가니시로 재활용하는 등 지속가능한 바 문화를 실천한다. 업장명도 '제로 웨이스트'의 준말. 한라봉, 참외 등 제철 과일로 재증류한 진은 이곳만의 시그너처 베이스다.

ZEST pursues a sustainable bar culture by making its own tonic water to reduce waste and by using fruit peels as garnish. The name of the bar is also short for "zero waste." The gin re-distilled with seasonal vegetables such as hallabong tangerine and Korean melon serves as its signature liquor base.

Address	서울시 강남구 도산대로55길 26, 1층 1F, 26, Dosan-daero 55-gil, Gangnam-gu, Seoul
Tel	010-3177-8801
Menu	Z&T ₩25,000 소이 캬라멜 Soy Caramel ₩25,000
Hours	평일 Weekdays 18:30-02:00, 주말 Weekends 15:00-02:00
◎	zest.seoul

바 & 펍 | Bar & Pub

찰스 H. 칵테일 바 Cocktail Bar
CHARLES H.

포시즌스 호텔 내에 은밀히 자리한 스피크이지 바다. 비밀 문을 열고 들어서면, 전 세계 다양한 칵테일을 즐겼던 미국 작가 찰스 H. 베이커의 흔적이 녹아 있는 공간에서 예술적인 칵테일을 맛볼 수 있다. 호텔 바만의 비할 데 없는 호스피탤러티는 덤이다.

CHARLES H. is a speakeasy bar that is accessible via a secret passageway within Four Seasons Hotel. Once you enter Charles H. through the secret path, you can taste the artistic cocktails in the bar inspired by American author Charles H. Baker Jr., who enjoyed a variety of cocktails all over the world. You can also enjoy the hotel bar's incomparable hospitality.

Address	서울시 종로구 새문안로 97, 포시즌스 호텔 서울 LL층(지하 1층) Floor LL (B1), Four Seasons Hotel Seoul, 97, Saemunan-ro, Jongno-gu, Seoul
Tel	02-6388-5500
Menu	맨해튼 플라이트 Manhattan Flight ₩32,000 미스 프리다 Miss Frida ₩30,000
Hours	18:00-01:30
ⓘ	charleshseoul

파인앤코 칵테일 바 Cocktail Bar
Pine & Co

신사동 골목에 숨겨져 있는 스피크이지 콘셉트의 칵테일 바다. 각종 대회에서 우승을 휩쓴 박범석, 홍두의 바텐더가 특색 있는 칵테일을 선보인다. 시그너처 메뉴로는 이화곡과 백곡균을 보리와 함께 우린 위스키에 탄산을 더한 '누룩'이 있다.

A speakeasy cocktail bar hidden in an alleyway of Sinsa-dong. Unique cocktails are presented by bartenders Park Beom-seok and Hong Du-ui, who have won multiple global contests. The signature cocktail is Nuruk, made with ehwagok and white koji mold infused in whiskey with barley and added to carbonated water.

Address	서울시 강남구 선릉로157길 33, 지하 1층 B1, 33, Seolleung-ro 157-gil, Gangnam-gu, Seoul
Tel	010-6817-0406
Menu	누룩 Nuruk ₩23,000 히노끼 Hinoki ₩23,000
Hours	19:00-02:00 월요일 휴무 Closed on Mondays
	pineandco_seoul

바 & 펍 | Bar & Pub

채식 맛집 50선
50 Plant-based

* 적합성(식물기반 메뉴 50% 이상), 다양성(다양한 카테고리), 이슈성(식물기반 식문화 확산을 위한 캠페인, 쿠킹클래스 등을 적극적으로 함)을 기준으로 선별했습니다.
* The selection was based on the criteria of conformity (plant-based menus should constitute at least 50%), diversity (diverse categories), and public interest (active in holding campaigns and cooking classes to disseminate the plant-based food culture).

공간 녹음
Nokum Space

남미 플랜트랩
Nammi Plant Lab

더브레드블루
THE BREAD BLUE

도반
Doban

두두리두팡
DUDURIDUPANG

드렁큰 비건
Drunken Vegan

레이지 파머스
LAZY FARMERS

로컬릿
local EAT

마지
Maji

마치래빗 샐러드
March rabbit Salad

마히나 비건 테이블
MAHINA VEGAN TABLE

몽크스델리
MONK's DELI

몽크스부처
MONK's BUTCHER

문쥬스
MOON JUICE

미건테이블
Migun Table

바이두부
by TOFU

발우공양
Balwoo Gongyang

밥풀꽃
Babpullkkot

베이스 이즈 나이스
base is nice

베제투스
Vegetus

비건마마
Vegan Mama

비건 앤 비욘드
Vegan & Beyond

비푸스
VFUS

산촌
Sanchon

소이로움
SOIROUM

스타일비건
STYLE VEGAN

슬런치 팩토리
Slunch Factory

식물성 도산
SikMulSung Dosan

앞으로의 빵집
appbbang

양출 서울
Yangchul Seoul

오뇽
oignon

오세계향
Osegyehyang

우부래도
ooh Breado

음 이터리&베이커리
UUUM EATERY & BAKERY

채근담 역삼점
Chegeundaam Yeoksam

천년식향
Millennial Dining

칙피스
chick peace

카멜스 키친
CAMEL'S KITCHEN

카무플라주
Camouflage

쿠소이
KUSoy

큔
Qyun

평상시
Pyeongsangshi

포리스트키친
Forest Kitchen

포포브레드
for four Bread

푸드더즈매터
FOOD DOES MATTER

플랜튜드
PLANTUDE

플랜트
PLANT

핀치 브런치바
pinch brunch bar

해밀
Haemil

흠마켓
hmm market

공간 녹음 양식 Western
Nokum Space

채광 좋고 녹음 짙은 테라스를 겸비한 레스토랑이다. 비건 테마 아래 커리, 파스타, 가지 덮밥, 버섯과 비건 대체육으로 만든 탕수육 등 다양한 카테고리의 요리를 선보인다. 라이브 공연을 감상하며 칵테일과 위스키를 즐길 수 있는 비밀스러운 공간도 갖추고 있다.

A restaurant with a well-lit terrace full of foliage. Under the vegan theme, the restaurant serves a wide range of dishes such as curry, pasta, stir-fried eggplant with rice, and tangsuyuk (originally deep-fried pork with sweet-and-sour sauce) made with mushrooms and vegan meat substitute. It also has a secluded space where you can see a live performance while enjoying cocktails and whiskey.

Address	서울시 강서구 공항대로 227 403호, 마곡센트럴타워 1차 Magok Central Tower 1-403, 227, Gonghang-daero, Gangseo-gu, Seoul
Tel	02-6953-6998
Menu	녹음 카레 Nokum Curry ₩17,000 가지 덮밥 Stir-fried Eggplant with Rice ₩17,000
Hours	11:30-15:00, 17:30-01:00, 월요일 휴무 Closed on Mondays
◎	nokumspace

채식 맛집 50선 | 50 Plant-based

남미 플랜트랩 양식 Western
Nammi Plant Lab

비건이 아니어도 맛있게 즐길 수 있는 음식을 모토로 한다. 채소를 적극 활용할 뿐 아니라 식물성 재료의 특징을 연구해 채소 기반 리코타 치즈나 크림을 만들고, 식물성 대체육을 활용한 버거와 미트볼 등 폭넓은 비건식을 선보인다.

Nammi Plant Lab's mission is to serve delicious dishes that even non-vegans can enjoy. The restaurant not only actively uses vegetables, but also studies the properties of plant-based ingredients. Based on such efforts, the restaurant makes its own vegetable-based ricotta cheese and cream. It presents a wide range of vegan dishes such as a burger and meatballs made with plant-based meat alternatives.

Address	서울시 서초구 방배천로4안길 55, 2층 2F, 55, Bangbaecheon-ro 4an-gil, Seocho-gu, Seoul
Tel	02-522-1276
Menu	베지터블 굴라쉬 Vegetable Goulash ₩10,500 치즈 야채 피자 Cheese & Veggie Pizza ₩15,000
Hours	월-금요일 Monday-Friday 12:00-16:00, 17:30-21:00 토·일요일 Saturday & Sunday 12:00-21:00
	nammiplantlab

더브레드블루 디저트 카페 Dessert Café
THE BREAD BLUE

쌀가루를 사용한 쌀낭시에, 두유와 얼그레이티로 풍부한 맛을 낸 파운드케이크, 비건 음료 등 엄선한 식물성 재료로 만든 메뉴를 준비한다. 직접 제작한 특수 매대는 빵의 수분 증발을 막고 비닐 사용을 최소화하기 위함이다.

THE BREAD BLUE makes a "ssalnancier" (rice financier) using rice flour, a pound cake richly flavored with soy milk and Earl Grey tea, and vegan beverages with select plant-based ingredients. It made its own display stand to prevent breads from losing moisture and to minimize the use of plastic.

Address	서울시 마포구 신촌로12다길 3, 1층 1F, 3, Sinchon-ro 12da-gil, Mapo-gu, Seoul
Tel	070-4128-0720
Menu	쌀낭시에 Ssalnancier ₩2,500 프리미엄 비건버거 Premium Vegan Burger ₩9,800
Hours	10:00-21:00
	thebreadblue_official

도반 사찰 음식 Korean Temple Dining
Doban

점심 밥상과 예약제 코스 요리에 주력하는 사찰 음식 전문점이다. 육류를 사용하지 않는 만큼 콩과 식물성 기름, 다양한 채소로 영양 균형을 맞추기 위해 각별히 신경 쓴다. 최소한의 천연 조미료와 장류를 사용해 담백하고 깔끔한 맛을 즐길 수 있다.

A Buddhist temple food specialty restaurant serving lunch and course meals by reservation. The restaurant gives extra attention to nutrition to replace meat balance by using beans, vegetable oils, and a variety of vegetables. You can enjoy clean flavors from the use of natural seasonings and Korean sauces in minimal amounts.

Address	서울시 서초구 마방로6길 7-27, 지하 1층 B1, 7-27, Mabang-ro 6-gil, Seocho-gu, Seoul
Tel	02-1644-1803
Menu	점심 특선(2인 이상) Lunch Special (min. 2 people) ₩11,000 B 코스(평일 저녁&주말, 3인 이상) Course B (Weekday dinner & Weekends, min. 3 people) ₩50,000
Hours	11:00~22:00
◉	doban_fnb

두두리두팡 디저트 카페 Dessert Café
DUDURIDUPANG

동물성 재료와 밀가루를 사용하지 않는 비건 글루텐 프리 디저트 카페. 갸또의 단맛은 사탕수수 설탕 대신 코코넛 슈거와 천연 감미료인 알룰로스, 그리고 재료 본연의 맛으로 구현한다. 텀블러나 디저트 용기 지참 시 할인받을 수 있다.

A vegan and gluten-free dessert café that does not use animal ingredients or wheat flour. The sweet flavor of gateau comes from coconut sugar, the natural sweetener allulose, and the original flavors of other ingredients instead of sugar from sugarcane. You can receive a discount for bringing your own tumbler or dessert container.

Address	서울시 마포구 월드컵로23길 19, 1층 1F, 19, World Cup-ro 23-gil, Mapo-gu, Seoul
Tel	070-8810-2379
Menu	비건 갸또 Vegan Gateau ₩9,600(변동) (varies) 오리지널 두라미수 Original Soy Milk Tiramisu ₩7,900
Hours	12:00-19:00 월-수요일 휴무 Closed on Mondays through Wednesdays
◎	duduri_dupang

채식 맛집 50선 | 50 Plant-based

드렁큰 비건 펍 Pub
Drunken Vegan

술을 사랑하는 비건들의 아지트로 통하는 곳이다. 동물성 성분을 제거한 자리를 리치와 레몬의 상큼 달달한 풍미로 채운 시그니처 소주와 칵테일, 비건 와인을 갖추고 있다. 두부 라자냐, 유린기 등의 안주 메뉴도 모두 비건식이다.

Drunken Vegan is well known as a favorite hangout for vegan liquor lovers. It has a variety of cocktails and vegan wines, including the signature soju sweetened and flavored with lychee and lemon instead of animal ingredients. It serves vegan side snacks such as bean curd lasagna and yuringi (based on deep-fried chicken in hot and sour soy sauce).

Address 서울시 마포구 와우산로30길 13, 101호
101, 13, Wausan-ro 30-gil, Mapo-gu, Seoul
Tel 070-7543-8101
Menu 드렁큰비건 시그니쳐 소주 Drunken Vegan's Signature Soju ₩12,000
비건 두부 라자냐 Vegan Bean Curd Lasagna ₩18,000
Hours 17:00-22:00
월·화요일 휴무 Closed on Mondays & Tuesdays

drunkenvegan101

레이지 파머스 양식 Western
LAZY FARMERS

이름과 달리 부지런한 요리사들이 재료의 특성을 연구한 비건식을 선보인다. 두부로 리코타 치즈를 만들고 새송이버섯으로 관자 식감을 구현하는 식이다. 고사리, 김 페스토 등 한국적인 재료를 양식에 접목해 개성 있는 요리를 완성한다.

ⓒ글로우서울

ⓒ글로우서울

In contrast with the restaurant's name, the vegan dishes are presented by diligent cooks based on their hard work to understand the characteristics of each ingredient. They make ricotta cheese using bean curd and achieve the texture of scallops using king oyster mushrooms. You can enjoy unique dishes incorporating Korean ingredients such as bracken and laver pesto into Western cuisine.

Address	서울시 용산구 회나무로35길 5, A동 Building A, 5, Hoenamu-ro 35-gil, Yongsan-gu, Seoul
Tel	070-8804-6301
Menu	캐슈넛 크림 미소 파스타 Cashew Nut Cream Miso Pasta ₩21,000 팔라펠과 참깨 후무스 Falafel & Sesame Seed Hummus ₩19,000
Hours	11:30–15:00, 17:00–21:30
◉	lazyfarmers2284

채식 맛집 50선 | 50 Plant-based

로컬릿 유러피언 European
local EAT

팜투테이블을 실천하는 남정석 셰프의 채식 기반 다이닝. 농부 시장이나 소규모 농장 등에서 수급한 로컬 식재료를 활용해 건강하면서도 맛있는 유러피언 요리를 선보인다. 백태콩으로 만든 후무스와 채소를 차곡차곡 쌓은 채소 테린이 시그너처 메뉴다.

It is a vegetarian-based restaurant by chef Nam Jeong-seok, who applies farm-to-table practices. The restaurant procures local ingredients from farmers' markets or small farms to serve healthy and delicious European dishes. Its signature dishes are Hummus made with white soybean and Vegetable Terrine made with layers of vegetables.

Address	서울시 성동구 한림말길 33, 2층 2F, 33, Hallimmal-gil, Seongdong-gu, Seoul
Tel	02-2282-1124
Menu	채소 테린 Vegetable Terrine ₩16,000 시금치 뇨끼 Spinach Gnocchi ₩19,000
Hours	11:00-15:00, 17:00-21:00, 주말 Weekends 11:00-21:00
◉	the_local_eater

마지
사찰 음식 Korean Temple Dining
Maji

사찰 음식을 바탕으로 한 채식 요리 전문점이다. 오신채를 쓰지 않고, 직접 담근 장과 무농약 채소를 활용한 자연 그대로의 맛을 식탁에 올린다. 배냉면, 호두만두 등 개성 있는 메뉴도 눈에 띈다. 대부분의 재료는 10년 이상 거래한 농가나 사찰에서 받는다.

A vegetarian restaurant specializing in Buddhist temple dishes. The restaurant presents the true flavors of nature, using handmade sauces and pesticide-free vegetables, excluding the five forbidden pungent herbs. It also serves some unique dishes such as Cold Buckwheat Noodles with Pear and Walnut Mandu. It procures most of the ingredients from farms and temples with whom it has been doing business for over 10 years.

Address	서울시 종로구 자하문로5길 19 19, Jahamun-ro 5-gil, Jongno-gu, Seoul
Tel	02-536-5228
Menu	고급 코스 Premium Course ₩40,000-60,000 런치·디너 세트 Lunch/Dinner Sets ₩21,000
Hours	11:30-15:00, 17:00-21:00 화요일 휴무 Closed on Tuesdays
W	www.templefood.com

채식 맛집 50선 | 50 Plant-based

마치래빗 샐러드 샐러드 Salad
March rabbit Salad

노란색 벽돌과 연두색 차양으로 외관부터 싱그러운 기운이 전해지는 샐러드 전문점이다. 10년 넘는 시간 동안 비건부터 일반식까지 건강한 식단을 제안해왔다. 밥 위에 두부, 버섯, 달걀 등 기호에 따라 토핑을 올려 먹는 라이스 볼이 대표 메뉴다.

A specialty salad shop whose yellow bricks and yellow-green awnings give a refreshing vibe. March rabbit Salad has been presenting a healthy diet including both vegan and non-vegan dishes for over 10 years. Its signature dish is a rice bowl where you can select toppings as you like, such as bean curd, mushroom, and egg.

Address 서울시 강남구 논현로153길 45
45, Nonhyeon-ro 153-gil, Gangnam-gu, Seoul
Tel 070-4531-4514
Menu 마치래빗 March Rabbit ₩9,900
스도 Stamina Rice Bowl ₩10,900
Hours 11:00-15:30, 17:30-21:00
◎ marchrabbitsalad

마히나 비건 테이블 이탤리언 Italian
MAHINA VEGAN TABLE

김홍록 현대미술 작가가 운영하는 곳으로 갤러리를 연상시키는 감각적인 공간에서 비건식을 즐길 수 있다. 벚꽃과 함께 숙성한 샬롯 피클, 비건 페페로니, 버건 번과 패티 등 접시에 담긴 모든 요소와 주류까지 100% 비건이다.

At this restaurant run by a contemporary artist Kim Hong-rok, you can enjoy vegan dishes in a sensuous space reminiscent of an art gallery. The restaurant serves 100% vegan dishes, including all ingredients on the plate, such as shallot pickles ripened with cherry blossoms, vegan pepperoni, vegan buns, and vegan patties, as well as all of the liquors.

Address	서울시 강남구 논현로175길 75, 2층 2F, 75, Nonhyeon-ro 175-gil, Gangnam-gu, Seoul
Tel	070-4105-5331
Menu	그린 스페셜 코스 Green Special Course ₩120,000 그릴드 파인애플 버거 Grilled Pineapple Burger ₩25,000
Hours	수-금요일 Wednesday-Friday 17:30-22:00 토·일요일 Saturday & Sunday 11:00-16:00, 17:00-22:00 월·화요일 휴무 Closed on Mondays & Tuesdays
	mahina_vegan_table

채식 맛집 50선 | 50 Plant-based

몽크스델리 양식 Western
MONK's DELI

비건들의 성지 <몽크스부처>에서 오픈한 곳이다. 델리 콘셉트에 걸맞게 수프와 구운 채소, 토스트, 샌드위치 등 가볍게 즐길 수 있는 일상 요리를 선보인다. 접시마다 똠얌 마요, 오렌지 소스 등 이곳만의 킥을 더한 것이 포인트다.

A restaurant opened by "MONK's BUTCHER", the so-called shrine of vegans. In line with its deli concept, it presents casual dishes such as soup, grilled vegetables, toast, and sandwiches. The restaurant adds unique kicks to its dishes, such as tom yum mayo and orange sauce.

Address	서울시 용산구 신흥로 57, 103호 103, 57, Sinheung-ro, Yongsan-gu, Seoul
Tel	02-795-1108
Menu	오렌지 치킨 라이스 Orange Chicken Rice ₩14,000 두부치킨버거 Bean Curd Chicken Burger ₩15,000
Hours	11:00-21:30 월요일 휴무 Closed on Mondays
	monksdeli

몽크스부처 양식 Western
MONK's BUTCHER

로메스코 소스를 곁들인 컬리플라워 스테이크, 노루궁뎅이버섯으로 만든 비건 강정 등 특색 있는 메뉴를 맛볼 수 있는 곳. 비건들의 성지로 통한다. 메인 요리뿐 아니라 비건 아이스크림 등 디저트까지 완벽한 비건식으로 만날 수 있다.

MONK's BUTCHER serves unique dishes such as cauliflower steak served with romesco sauce and vegan deep-fried lion's mane mushrooms. It is known as a shrine for vegans. You can enjoy a perfect vegan meal from the main dishes to the desserts including vegan ice cream.

Address	서울시 용산구 이태원로 228-1, 3 & 4층
	3 & 4F, 228-1, Itaewon-ro, Yongsan-gu, Seoul
Tel	02-790-1108
Menu	컬리플라워 스테이크 Cauliflower Steak ₩18,000
	비건 강정 Vegan Deep-fried Lion's Mane Mushrooms ₩18,000
Hours	월-목요일 Monday-Thursday 17:00-23:00
	금-일요일 Friday-Sunday 11:00-15:00, 17:00-23:00
	monksbutcher

문쥬스 브런치 & 와인 바 Brunch & Wine Bar
MOON JUICE

채소와 발효 요소를 적극 활용해온 <와일드플라워> 조은빛 셰프가 오픈한 곳. 낮에는 비건과 베지테리언 옵션의 브런치를, 저녁에는 내추럴 와인과 어울리는 발효 테마의 요리, 화덕 피자를 즐기기 좋다. 피자 역시 베지테리언 옵션을 갖추고 있다.

A brunch and wine bar opened by chef Jo Eun-bit of "Wild Flower", who has been actively applying vegetables and fermented ingredients to her dishes. It is a good place to enjoy vegan or vegetarian brunch dishes during the day and fermentation-themed dishes and oven-baked pizzas with natural wine at night. It offers vegetarian options for pizzas as well.

Address	서울시 서초구 서초대로25길 33, 1층 1F, 33 Seocho-daero 25-gil, Seocho-gu, Seoul
Tel	02-6449-3002
Menu	세비체 Ceviche ₩17,000 수퍼문 Super Moon ₩19,000
Hours	11:30-15:00, 18:00-22:30 화·수요일 휴무 Closed on Tuesdays & Wednesdays
◎	moonjuice.seoul

미건테이블 _{한식} Korean
Migun Table

음식도 약처럼 몸을 치유할 수 있다는 모토 아래 건강한 밥상을 차린다. 장흥 고대미 쌀밥, 채소의 뿌리, 줄기, 잎, 열매를 고루 활용한 나물 반찬, 장아찌 등 80% 이상을 채소로 구성했다. 미리 예약하면 채식 상차림도 가능하다.

Migun Table serves healthy dishes with the motto of foods that can heal the body like medicine. Over 80% of its dishes are made using vegetables, such as Jangheung Godaemi rice, pickled vegetables, and side dishes made with the roots, stems, leaves, and fruits of vegetables. You can enjoy a vegetarian set menu if you make a reservation in advance.

Address	서울시 광진구 동일로 260 260, Dongil-ro, Gwangjin-gu, Seoul
Tel	0507-1409-0004
Menu	미건 치유밥상 Migun Healing Set Menu ₩25,000 미건 특선밥상 Migun Special Set Menu ₩35,000
Hours	10:00-22:00
◉	migun_table

채식 맛집 50선 | 50 Plant-based

바이두부 샐러드 Salad
by TOFU

두부와 두유를 주제로 샐러드, 랩, 샌드위치를 선보인다. 오븐에 구운 두부강정, 브로콜리, 퀴노아 샐러드를 조합한 브로콜리 두부강정은 맛과 포만감을 모두 잡은 스테디셀러 메뉴. 다회 용기를 가져와 포장하면 10% 할인 혜택도 제공한다.

This restaurant presents salads, wraps, and sandwiches under the theme of bean curd and soy milk. The Salad Ball with Broccoli and Deep-fried Bean Curd, the combination of broccoli, oven-baked bean curd, and quinoa salad, is a delicious and hearty steady seller. You will get a 10% discount if you bring your own reusable container for the food.

Address 서울시 용산구 소월로20길 10
10, Sowol-ro 20-gil, Yongsan-gu, Seoul
Tel 070-8228-7019
Menu 브로콜리 두부강정 샐러드볼
Salad Ball with Broccoli and Deep-fried Bean Curd ₩11,000
에그레스 샌드위치 Eggless Sandwich ₩9,500
Hours 09:30-17:00
화·수요일 휴무 Closed on Tuesdays & Wednesdays
bytofu_hbc

발우공양 사찰 음식 Korean Temple Dining
Balwoo Gongyang

ⓟ 🍴 🌱

대한불교 조계종에서 직접 운영하고 있는 사찰 음식 전문 레스토랑. 유기농 채소를 주요 식재료로 사용하며, 직접 담근 전통 장과 최소한의 양념만을 더해 속이 편안한 코스 요리를 내놓는다. 별실로 된 아늑한 공간에서 수행 음식 문화를 음미할 수 있다.

A restaurant specializing in temple dishes, run by the Jogye Order of Korean Buddhism. You can enjoy a temple food course meal consisting of easily digestible dishes made with mainly organic vegetables, seasoned with handmade traditional sauces and minimal seasonings. You can experience the food culture of spiritual cultivation in a cozy private room.

Address	서울시 종로구 우정국로 56, 5층 5F, 56, Ujeongguk-ro, Jongno-gu, Seoul
Tel	010-2956-3493, 02-733-2081
Menu	원식 코스 메뉴 Won Course ₩45,000 마음식 코스 메뉴 Maeum Course ₩65,000
Hours	11:30-13:20(런치 1부) (Lunch 1), 13:30-14:50(런치 2부) (Lunch 2), 18:00-21:30 일요일 휴무 Closed on Sundays
📷	balwoogongyang_official

채식 맛집 50선 | 50 Plant-based

밥풀꽃 한식 Korean
Babpullkkot

채식, 로컬, 친환경 세 가지를 원칙으로 삼는다. 탄소발자국을 줄이기 위해 가까운 농장과 마을에서 대부분의 재료를 수급한다. 계절의 향기를 고스란히 담은 풀꽃 비빔밥, 채수를 끓여 만든 채개장 등 소박하지만 정성 가득한 한 끼를 선사한다.

Babpullkkot follows three principles: vegetarian diet, local ingredients, and eco-friendliness. It procures most of its ingredients from nearby farms and villages in order to reduce its carbon footprint. It serves simple but heartfelt dishes such as Flower Bibimbap delivering the scent of the season and Spicy Veggie Soup made from vegetable broth.

Address	서울시 은평구 연서로15길 8, 1층 1F, 8, Yeonseo-ro 15-gil, Eunpyeong-gu, Seou
Tel	02-387-1129
Menu	풀꽃 비빔밥 Flower Bibimbap ₩9,000 채개장 Spicy Veggie Soup ₩9,000
Hours	11:30-14:30
〇	babpullkkot

베이스 이즈 나이스 모던 한식 Modern Korean
base is nice

다양한 방식으로 채소 본연의 맛과 향을 살린 채소 중심의 다이닝이다. 삶고 데치는 한식 조리법에서 벗어나, 말리거나 굽거나 훈연하는 등 다양한 조리법을 접목한 것이 특징. 튀긴 청무와 구운 옥수수 등 각종 채소를 밥 위에 얹은 채소밥은 익숙하면서도 색다르다.

A vegetarian-based restaurant that presents the original flavors and aromas of vegetables in diverse ways. The restaurant uses a variety of techniques such as drying, grilling, and smoking instead of adhering to traditional Korean methods such as boiling and parboiling. Vegetable rice made with steamed rice and topped with various vegetables such as deep-fried radish and baked corn is familiar yet unique.

Address	서울시 마포구 도화2길 20 20, Dohwa 2-gil, Mapo-gu, Seoul
Tel	010-9617-6724
Menu	바삭 청무와 옥수수 밥 Crunchy Radish and Corn Rice ₩20,000 무화과를 올린 발효버터 햇우엉구이 밥 Fresh Grilled Burdock Root Rice with Fermented Butter and Fig ₩20,000
Hours	11:30–15:00 월요일 휴무 Closed on Mondays
◎	baseisnice_seoul

채식 맛집 50선 | 50 Plant-based

베제투스 유러피언 European
Vegetus

해방촌에 위치한 식물성 요리 전문점이다. 대표 메뉴인 베제투스버거는 시중의 햄버거와 달리 렌틸콩과 양파, 버섯으로 만든 패티를 사용해 고소한 맛과 부드러운 식감을 살렸다. 바질과 마늘을 혼합한 페스토, 스리라차 마요네즈 등의 소스는 감칠맛을 더하는 요소.

A vegetarian restaurant located in Haebangchon. The signature dish, Vegetus Burger, features a savory flavor and soft texture for its patty made with lentils, onions, and mushrooms. Its special sauces such as basil and garlic-mixed pesto and sriracha mayo upgrade the taste of the dishes.

Address 서울시 용산구 신흥로 59
59, Sinheung-ro, Yongsan-gu, Seoul
Tel 070-8824-5959
Menu 라자냐 Lasagna ₩17,000
베제투스버거 Vegetus Burger ₩14,000
Hours 평일 Weekdays 12:00-15:00, 17:00-21:30, 주말 Weekends 12:00-21:30
vegetuskr

비건마마 디저트 카페 Dessert Café
Vegan Mama

흑임자, 쑥, 제주 레몬 등 한국 재료를 다채롭게 활용해 비건 디저트를 선보인다. 수제 과일잼을 듬뿍 넣은 현미 스콘은 담백하면서도 달콤하다. 두유 요거트와 그래놀라를 사용한 비건 요거트 볼 등 건강한 한 끼를 위한 선택지가 다양하다.

Vegan Mama presents vegan desserts using a diverse range of Korean ingredients such as black sesame, mugwort, and Jeju lemon. Its brown rice scone filled with handmade fruit jam has a plain but sweet flavor. It serves a variety of healthy meal choices, such as a vegan yogurt ball made with soy milk yogurt and granola.

Address	서울시 관악구 봉천로 457-1, 1층
	1F, 457-1, Bongcheon-ro, Gwanak-gu, Seoul
Tel	010-2653-7204
Menu	단호박 쌀케이크 Pumpkin Rice Cake ₩6,000
	흑임자 찹쌀 타르트 Black Sesame and Sweet Rice Tart ₩6,000
Hours	12:00-23:00
	일요일 휴무 Closed on Sundays
◉	veganmamabakery

비건 앤 비욘드 양식 Western
Vegan & Beyond

영국 전통 고기 파이인 셰퍼드 파이도, 햄버그 스테이크도 모두 비건으로 즐길 수 있다.
비건 고기와 국내산 유기농, 무농약 인증 재료를 사용한 든든한 요리들을 선보인다.
커피와 함께 브런치로, 비건 와인과 함께 안주로 즐겨도 좋다.

You can enjoy shepherd's pie, which is a traditional British meat pie, and hamburg steak all as vegan versions. The restaurant prepares hearty dishes using plant-based meat substitutes and Korean organic and pesticide-free ingredients. You can enjoy them as brunch with a cup of coffee or as a side for vegan wine.

Address 서울시 서대문구 연희맛로 33, 2층
2F, 33, Yeonhuimat-ro, Seodaemun-gu, Seoul
Tel 070-7543-9139
Menu 셰퍼드 파이 Shepherd's Pie ₩11,500
치지 슈프림 프라이즈 Cheezy Supreme Fries ₩13,500
Hours 11:00-22:00
화요일 휴무 Closed on Tuesdays

veganandbeyondkr

비푸스 브런치 카페 Brunch Café
VFUS

비건식을 즐길 수 있는 레스토랑 및 카페이자 그로서리를 겸하고 있다. 튀긴 두부, 쫄깃한 뇨끼 등 식감을 강조한 재료를 다채로운 채소와 조합해 지루하지 않은 한 접시를 제안한다. 한편에서는 식물성 원료만을 사용한 세계 각국의 다양한 식재료를 구매할 수 있다.

VFUS is a vegan restaurant, café, and grocery. It presents intriguing dishes by combining ingredients with an emphasis on textures, such as deep-fried bean curd and chewy gnocchi, with a wide range of vegetables. You can also purchase a variety of purely plant-based ingredients from all over the world in the grocery.

Address	서울시 서초구 서운로26길 11, 1층 1F, 11, Seoun-ro 26-gil, Seocho-gu, Seoul
Tel	02-6092-8575
Menu	그릴드 베지 뇨끼 Grilled Veggie Gnocchi ₩14,900 크리스피 두부 Crispy Bean Curd ₩11,900
Hours	카페&그로서리 Café & Grocery 11:00-20:00 레스토랑 Restaurant 11:00-14:30, 16:30-19:30 일요일 휴무 Closed on Sundays
◉	vfus_seoul

산촌 사찰 음식 Korean Temple Dining
Sanchon

인사동 부근의 사찰 음식 전문점으로, 산속에서 자라는 채소와 나물을 주재료로 한다. 야생초를 활용한 한식 반상 차림을 비롯해 다양한 계절 반찬을 맛볼 수 있다. 한옥 구조의 공간 곳곳에 놓인 식물과 사찰 소품들로 고즈넉한 분위기를 자아낸다.

A Buddhist temple food restaurant located in Insa-dong. The restaurant uses mainly wild vegetables and edible greens. It serves Korean set menus made with wild vegetables and other various seasonal side dishes. Plants and Buddhist temple items placed in this hanok restaurant create a peaceful atmosphere.

Address	서울시 종로구 인사동길 30-13 30-13, Insadong-gil, Jongno-gu, Seoul
Tel	02-735-0312
Menu	산촌 정식(점심) Sanchon Set Menu (Lunch) ₩29,000 산촌 정식(저녁) Sanchon Set Menu (Dinner) ₩29,000
Hours	12:00-20:30
Ⓦ	www.sanchon.com

소이로움 양식 Western
SOIROUM

가까이는 주변의 농가, 멀리는 지구, 그리고 우리 몸에 이로운 먹거리를 추구한다. 친환경 채소, 공정무역 견과류, 사회적 기업의 원두, 농가 직거래 차를 사용한다. 삶은 콩을 발효해 만드는 템페조림덮밥이 별미로 꼽힌다.

SOIROUM pursues foods beneficial to nearby farms, the earth, and the body. It uses eco-friendly vegetables, fair trade nuts, coffee beans produced by social enterprises, and tea procured directly from farms. Its signature dish is Braised Tempeh with Rice made with fermented boiled soybeans.

Address	서울시 종로구 필운대로 41, 1층 1F, 41, Pirundae-ro, Jongno-gu, Seoul
Tel	02-586-8088
Menu	템페조림덮밥 Braised Tempeh with Rice ₩13,000 베지함박플레이트 Veggie Hamburg Plate ₩14,000
Hours	화-금요일 Tuesday-Friday 11:30-15:00, 17:00-20:00 토·일요일 Saturday & Sunday 11:30-20:00 월요일 휴무 Closed on Mondays
	so_iroum

채식 맛집 50선 | 50 Plant-based

스타일비건 아메리칸 American
STYLE VEGAN

밀크 셰이크 & 버거라는 검증된 조합을 비건으로 풀어냈다. 옥수수 전분 추출 성분으로 만든 생분해성 용기를 사용하는 등 친환경적인 방법을 모색한다. 식물성 참치, 두부텐더 등 가정에서 요리에 활용할 수 있는 비건 식료품도 구매할 수 있다.

STYLE VEGAN presents the vegan version of the proven combination of milkshake and burger. It seeks eco-friendly practices such as biodegradable containers made from corn starch. You can also buy some vegan groceries such as plant-based tuna and bean curd tenders that you can easily cook at home.

Address	서울시 강남구 선릉로135길 6, 2층
	2F, 6, Seolleung-ro 135-gil, Gangnam-gu, Seoul
Tel	1800-2361
Menu	클래식 비건치즈버거 Classic Vegan Cheeseburger ₩14,500
	밀크쉐이크 Milkshake ₩6,000
Hours	11:00-22:00
	stylevegankr

슬런치 팩토리 유러피언 European
Slunch Factory

피자와 파스타, 수프, 덮밥 등 대중적인 메뉴를 식물성 재료로 탈바꿈했다. 락토오보, 페스코, 폴로, 그리고 비건까지 단계별 채식이 가능하다. 피자는 기본적으로 락토 베이스의 레시피지만 비건 치즈로 대체할 수 있다.

Slunch Factory makes popular dishes such as pizza, pasta, soup, and rice bowl using plant-based ingredients. It offers different types of vegetarian diet options that include lacto-ovo vegetarian, pescetarian, pollotarian, and vegan. Although pizza is a fundamentally lacto-based recipe, vegan cheese can be used instead.

Address	서울시 마포구 와우산로3길 38
	38, Wausan-ro 3-gil, Mapo-gu, Seoul
Tel	02-6367-9870
Menu	가지 시금치 파스타 Eggplant & Spinach Pasta ₩19,000
	아보카도 가지 쥬키니 피자 Avocado, Eggplant, and Zucchini Pizza ₩24,000
Hours	10:00-23:00
◎	slunch_factory

채식 맛집 50선 | 50 Plant-based

식물성 도산 디저트 카페 Dessert Café
SikMulSung Dosan

스마트팜 스타트업 엔씽의 카페 겸 쇼룸이다. 직접 수경재배한 채소로 만든 샐러드는 취향에 따라 드레싱을 선택할 수 있다. 대표 메뉴인 비건 바타비아 두부면 샐러드의 추천 드레싱은 비건 바질 페스토. 완두콩 두유로 만든 라테류도 인기다.

A café and showroom of "N.THING", a smart farm startup. The vegetables are grown using hydroponics for the salad dishes, and you can choose a dressing to fit your own taste. Vegan basil pesto is a recommended dressing for the signature dish, the Vegan Batavia Lettuce Salad with Bean Curd Noodles. The options for lattes made with pea milk are popular as well.

Address	서울시 강남구 압구정로42길 54, 1층 1F, 54, Apgujeong-ro 42-gil, Gangnam-gu, Seoul
Tel	070-4943-2144
Menu	비건 바타비아 두부면 샐러드 Vegan Batavia Lettuce Salad with Bean Curd Noodles ₩10,900 식물성 화이트 Vegetable White ₩7,000
Hours	11:00-22:00
	sikmulsung_official

앞으로의 빵집 디저트 카페 Dessert Café
appbbang

지역 농산물의 맛을 디저트에 담아낸다. 전남 영암의 고구마, 강화 쑥, 서산 만차랑 단호박 모두 발품을 마다 않고 찾은 재료들이다. 버터, 우유, 달걀은 물론 흰 밀가루, 흰 설탕, 흰 소금, 흰쌀, GMO, 방부제와 색소를 쓰지 않는 것을 원칙으로 한다.

This café makes its desserts using the flavors of local agricultural products. After all the legwork to find quality ingredients, the staffs found sweet potato from Yeongam in Jeonnam, mugwort from Ganghwado island, and Mancharang pumpkin from Seosan. They do not use white flour, white sugar, white salt, white rice, GMO crops, preservatives, or colors, as well as butter, milk, or eggs.

Address	서울시 종로구 삼일대로32가길 29-1
	29-1, Samil-daero 32ga-gil, Jongno-gu, Seou
Tel	010-6662-2943
Menu	단호박 모찌 타르트 Pumpkin Mochi Tart ₩6,000
	쑥무화과 파운드 Mugwort & Fig Pound Cake ₩4,800
Hours	금·토요일 Friday & Saturday 13:00-20:00
	일-목요일 휴무 Closed on Sundays through Thursdays

 apbbang

채식 맛집 50선 | 50 Plant-based

양출 서울 와인 바 Wine Bar
Yangchul Seoul

채소를 주인공으로 끌어올린 요리와 그에 어울리는 와인을 즐길 수 있는 곳이다. 맛과 비주얼 모두 메인 채소의 매력을 드러내는 데 집중한다. 매주 농장에서 수급하는 제철 채소에 맞춰 메뉴를 구성하기 때문에 변화무쌍한 재미가 있다.

Yangchul Seoul serves dishes where vegetables are the main ingredients and that you can enjoy with well-paired wine. It focuses on emphasizing the main vegetable ingredients in terms of both flavor and presentation. Its dishes change often since it serves different dishes depending on the seasonal vegetables procured directly from farms every week.

Address	서울시 강남구 언주로135길 34 34, Eonju-ro 135-gil, Gangnam-gu, Seoul
Tel	02-547-4420
Menu	컬리플라워(변동) Cauliflower (varies) ₩14,000 토마토 양파(변동) Tomato & Onion (varies) ₩13,000
Hours	19:00-22:00 일요일 휴무 Closed on Sundays
◎	yangchulseoul

오농 프렌치 French
oignon

해산물과 채소를 사용한 페스코 베지테리언 코스를 선보인다. 아뮈즈, 메인 요리인 제철 생선 스테이크, 디저트 구성의 런치 5코스, 디너 6코스다. 실내는 오픈 키친&바 구조로 식재료와 조리법에 대해 셰프와 대화를 나누는 즐거움도 있다.

The restaurant presents pescetarian course meals made with seafood and vegetables. Lunch and dinner consist of five and six courses, respectively, including amuse-bouche, seasonal fish steak as a main dish, and dessert. Its open kitchen and bar are another feature of the place, where you can talk about ingredients and recipes while enjoying a course meal.

Address	서울시 강남구 압구정로4길 13-4, 1층 1F, 13-4, Apgujeong-ro 4-gil, Gangnam-gu, Seoul
Tel	010-9033-9187
Menu	런치 테이스팅 코스 Lunch Tasting Course ₩65,000 디너 오농 코스 Dinner Oignon Course ₩88,000
Hours	수-금요일 Wednesday-Friday 12:00-14:00, 19:00-22:00 토·일요일 Saturday & Sunday 12:00-14:00, 18:00-22:00 월·화요일 휴무 Closed on Mondays and Tuesdays
	oignon_seoul

채식 맛집 50선 | 50 Plant-based

오세계향 한식 Korean
Osegyehyang

채식 베테랑이 2007년 오픈한 음식점이다. 된장들깨시래기찜 등의 한식, 비건 자장면과 버섯 중화탕면, 비건 떡볶이 등의 분식까지 30여 가지 폭넓은 메뉴로 다양한 기호를 충족한다. 밑반찬까지 모두 비건으로 제공하며 무오신채 옵션도 있다.

This restaurant was opened in 2007 by a highly experienced vegetarian. The chef serves around 30 different dishes, including Soybean Paste and Perilla Seed Stew with Dried Radish Leaves, vegan noodles in black bean sauce, noodle soup with mushrooms, and vegan tteokbokki. There is only vegan dishes, including side dishes, and you can also choose an option without the five forbidden pungent herbs (Buddhist principle).

Address	서울시 종로구 인사동12길 14-5
	14-5, Insadong 12-gil, Jongno-gu, Seoul
Tel	02-735-7171
Menu	된장들깨시래기찜
	Soybean Paste and Perilla Seed Stew with Dried Radish Leaves ₩10,000
	불구이쌈밥 Vegetarian Grill with Leaf Wraps and Rice ₩12,000
Hours	11:30-16:00, 17:00-21:00
Ⓦ	www.go5.co.kr

우부래도
베이커리 카페 Bakery Café
ooh Breado

글루텐 프리 여부, 견과류와 두유 등 알레르기 유발 가능 성분 유무를 꼼꼼하게 기록한 표로 신뢰감을 더하는 빵집. 유지방을 사용하지 않는 만큼 양양의 쑥, 당진 팥, 단호박 등 맛 좋은 원재료를 듬뿍 넣어 맛을 살린다.

The bakery provides a checklist for potentially allergenic ingredients such as gluten, nuts, and soy milk, adding to customer trust. It also excludes the use of butterfat. The flavor of desserts will captivate your taste buds as they are made with healthy ingredients such as Yangyang mugwort, Dangjin red beans, and pumpkin.

Address	서울시 동작구 상도로37길 3 3, Sangdo-ro 37-gil, Dongjak-gu, Seoul
Tel	070-7543-0599
Menu	단호박큐브 Pumpkin Cube ₩6,000 홍국단팥빵 Hongguk Bun with Sweet Red Bean Filling ₩3,000
Hours	10:30-21:00 월요일 휴무 Closed on Mondays
	ooh_breado

음 이터리 & 베이커리 양식, 아시안 Western, Asian
UUUM EATERY & BAKERY

자가제면한 글루텐 프리 메밀면, 콜리플라워로 만든 피자 도우 등 재료 하나하나 공을 들인다. 허브와 다양한 버섯으로 만든 뒥셀 패티 샌드위치는 비건, 논비건에게 모두 인기 있는 대표 메뉴. 메뉴 대부분 비건과 글루텐 프리 옵션을 갖추고 있다.

This bakery puts effort into all of its ingredients, such as gluten-free buckwheat noodles made with their own recipe and cauliflower pizza dough. The Duxelles Patty Sandwich made with herbs and a variety of mushrooms is popular with both vegans and non-vegans. Most of the menu features vegan and gluten-free options.

Address 서울시 강남구 논현로28길 47, 1층
1F, 47, Nonhyeon-ro 28-gil, Gangnam-gu, Seoul
Tel 02-572-2023
Menu 뒥셀 비건 시그니처 Duxelles Vegan Signature ₩12,900
지중해식 후무스 샐러드 Mediterranean Hummus Salad ₩11,900
Hours 11:00-15:00, 17:30-21:00
월·화요일 휴무 Closed on Mondays & Tuesdays

uuumseoul

채근담 역삼점 한식 Korean
Chegeundaam Yeoksam

버섯 우엉 들깨탕, 자연송이 마구이 등 계절마다 가장 맛있는 식재료로 채식 코스를 구성한다. 영양밥과 된장찌개, 두텁떡 디저트 등 한국의 대표적인 미식을 채식으로 경험하기 좋다. 별실이 마련되어 있어 프라이빗한 식사를 즐길 수 있다.

Chaegeundam Yeoksam offers vegetarian course meals with the most delicious seasonal ingredients, including perilla seed soup with mushrooms and burdock root and wild pine mushrooms and grilled yam. It is a good place to experience popular Korean dishes with vegetarian options, including nutritious steamed rice, soybean paste jjigae, and rice cake dessert with nut filling. The restaurant offers separate rooms for a private dining experience.

Address	서울시 강남구 테헤란로 152, 지하 1층 B1, 152, Teheran-ro, Gangnam-gu, Seoul
Tel	02-569-7165
Menu	평일 점심 Weekday Lunch ₩38,500–68,500 평일 저녁&주말 Weekday Dinner & Weekends ₩68,500–125,000
Hours	11:30–14:30, 17:30–21:30 일요일 휴무 Closed on Sundays
Ⓦ	www.chaegeundaam.com

채식 맛집 50선 | 50 Plant-based

천년식향 와인 바 Wine Bar
Millennial Dining

미국 로푸드 요리사 자격증을 취득한 안백린 셰프의 다이닝 바. 자연 재배한 허브를 산지 직송으로 수급받고 거의 모든 채소는 5시간 이상 저온 조리한다. 로스팅한 연시, 핑크 목이 피클 등 30여 가지 재료로 만든 퍼시몬 세비체는 채소의 새로운 면을 발견하게 한다.

A wine bar by US-certified raw food chef Ahn Baek-rin. She procures herbs grown by natural agricultural techniques directly from farms and cooks almost all vegetables at low temperature for over five hours. Persimmon Ceviche, made with around 30 ingredients including roasted soft persimmon and pink jelly ear pickles, will show you a new side of vegetables.

Address 서울시 서초구 효령로 316-1, 3층
3F, 316-1, Hyoryeong-ro, Seocho-gu, Seoul
Tel 010-6323-7231
Menu 퍼시몬 세비체 Persimmon Ceviche ₩22,000
레드 비트 라비올리 Red Beet Ravioli ₩24,000
Hours 월-금요일 Monday-Friday 18:00-22:00
토·일요일 Saturday & Sunday 12:30-15:30, 18:00-22:00

millennial_dining

칙피스 지중해 Mediterranean
chick peace

지중해와 중동풍 요리를 선보이는 곳. 식물성 재료 위주로 구성한 메뉴는 풍성한 맛과 양을 자랑하면서도 속이 편안하다. 후무스와 타히니 소스로 맛을 낸 비건 샐러드, 팔라펠 라이스는 오픈 초기부터 꾸준한 인기를 유지 중이다.

Chick peace serves Mediterranean and Middle Eastern dishes. Its hearty dishes made mainly with plant-based ingredients are both delicious and easily digestible. Vegan Salad and Falafel Rice served with hummus and tahini sauce have been popular since its opening.

Address	서울시 강남구 강남대로152길 69 69, Gangnam-daero 152-gil, Gangnam-gu, Seoul
Tel	02-6956-6780
Menu	비건 샐러드 Vegan salad ₩11,500 팔라펠 라이스 Falafel Rice ₩11,500
Hours	11:30-20:30
	chickpeace.kr

카멜스 키친 타이|Thai
CAMEL'S KITCHEN

태국 요리를 비건식으로 즐길 수 있는 곳이다. 똠얌꿍, 팟타이 등 페스코 단계의 요리가 주를 이루지만 대부분 비건식으로 대체 가능하다. 표고 플라워 후라이드 정식, 네 가지 버섯 볶음밥처럼 본래 비건으로 완성한 메뉴도 다양하다.

This restaurant offers vegan versions of Thai dishes. It serves mainly pescetarian dishes such as tom yum goong and pad thai, but most of its dishes can also be ordered as vegan. Its vegan menu is also diverse, with dishes such as Deep-fried Oak Mushroom & Cauliflower Set Menu and fried rice with four types of mushrooms.

Address 서울시 마포구 포은로 52-1, 2호
2, 52-1, Poeun-ro, Mapo-gu, Seoul
Tel 02-6326-3200
Menu 표고 플라워 후라이드 정식
Deep-fried Oak Mushroom & Cauliflower Set Menu ₩14,000
팟타이 Pad Thai ₩12,000
Hours 11:00-24:00
camel__kitchen

카무플라주
미국식 중식 American Chinese

Camouflage

정체를 들키지 않고 꾸민다는 뜻의 업장명처럼 미국식 중화요리의 맛과 모양새를 제대로 살렸다. 치킨 요리는 콩 치킨으로 대체하고 비건 새우를 사용한다. 두부와 버섯 등 갖가지 채소와 견과류로만 이루어진 요리도 다양하게 준비되어 있다.

As its name suggests, literally meaning hiding something without being caught, the restaurant presents the original flavors and presentations of American Chinese dishes. Soy meat is used to replace the meat in chicken dishes, and vegan shrimp is used for others. It also offers a variety of dishes made only with nuts and vegetables such as bean curd and mushrooms.

Address	서울시 용산구 이태원로26길 19, 2층 2F, 19, Itaewon-ro 26-gil, Yongsan-gu, Seoul
Tel	010-3557-3222
Menu	오렌지 치킨 Orange Chicken ₩12,500 쿵파오 치킨 Kung Pao Chicken ₩12,500
Hours	11:00-24:00
	camouflage_restaurant

쿠소이 디저트 카페 Dessert Café
KUSoy

첨가물 없이 100% 콩으로 만든 두부와 두유를 판매하는 젊은 감각의 카페. 두부로 만든 케이크와 쿠키 등의 디저트, 브런치, 음료도 있다. 두유 막걸리 쉐이크는 채식주의자가 아니더라도 이곳을 찾게 만드는 인기 메뉴다.

A café with a young vibe that offers additive-free bean curd and soy milk made with 100% soybeans. It also serves beverages, brunch dishes, and desserts such as cakes and cookies made with bean curd. Soy Milk Makgeolli Shake is a popular beverage with both vegans and non-vegans.

Address	서울시 성동구 한림말길 33, 지하 1층 B1, 33, Hallimmal-gil, Seongdong-gu, Seoul
Tel	02-466-7201
Menu	매쉬두 케이크 Mashdu Cake ₩7,000-8,000 쿠소이 두부 KUSoy Bean Curd ₩5,000
Hours	11:00-23:00 월요일 휴무 Closed on Mondays
	kusoy.official

큔 그로서리 카페 Grocery Café
Qyun

그로서리와 카페로 운영되는 서촌의 발효 식품 음식점. 다양한 발효 기법을 응용한 채소 중심의 요리와 건강 음료를 즐길 수 있다. 공간 한편의 '큔상점'에서는 삼발 토마토소스, 알알이 머스터드 피클, 금귤 발효 소금 등의 발효 조미료와 소스를 판매하고 있다.

A fermented food restaurant in Seochon, which is both a grocery store and café. You can enjoy healthy beverages and vegetable dishes made with a variety of fermentation techniques. Qyun Grocery Store, located in the corner of the restaurant, sells fermented seasonings and sauces such as sambal tomato sauce, mustard pickles, and fermented kumquat salt.

Address	서울시 종로구 자하문로26길 17-2, 1층 1F, 17-2, Jahamun-ro 26-gil, Jongno-gu, Seoul
Tel	010-3707-3711
Menu	구운 채소와 비건발효버터 커리 Grilled Vegetables with Fermented Vegan Butter Curry ₩16,000 템페와 삼발토마토소스 핫 샌드위치 Tempeh Sambal Tomato Sauce Hot Sandwich ₩9,000
Hours	11:00–16:00 월·화요일 휴무 Closed on Mondays & Tuesdays
	grocery_cafe_qyun

채식 맛집 50선 | 50 Plant-based

평상시 디저트 카페 Dessert Café
Pyeongsangshi

보통의 디저트에서 느낄 수 있는 달콤함과 촉촉함을 식물성 재료로 구현하기 위해 노력을 쏟았다. 대표 메뉴인 당근 케이크는 비정제 원당, 두유, 바닐라빈을 사용한다. 옥수수 푸딩 케이크, 무화과 얼그레이 케이크처럼 계절의 흐름을 느낄 수 있는 메뉴도 매달 선보인다.

This dessert café makes the effort to achieve the sweetness and moistness of regular non-vegan desserts while using only plant-based ingredients. Its signature dish, Carrot Cake, is made using unrefined raw sugar, soy milk, and vanilla bean. It presents new seasonal desserts every month, such as corn pudding cake and fig and Earl Grey cake.

Address	서울시 강동구 고덕로20길 26, 1층 1F, 26, Godeok-ro 20-gil, Gangdong-gu, Seoul
Tel	070-7655-0005
Menu	당근 케이크 Carrot Cake ₩6,500 계절과일 두부 치즈 타르트 Seasonal Fruit Bean Curd Cheese Tart ₩7,000
Hours	11:00-19:00 월-수요일 휴무 Closed on Mondays through Wednesdays
	pyeongsangshi

포리스트키친 이노베이티브 Innovative
Forest Kitchen

식탁 위의 지속가능성을 추구하는 프리미엄 비건 다이닝. 뉴욕 미쉐린 레스토랑 출신의 김태형 총괄 셰프가 제철 재료와 대체육을 활용해 코스 요리를 선보인다. 주된 식재료인 채소류는 파주의 유기농 직영 농장에서 매일 아침 배달 받는다.

A premium vegan restaurant pursuing food sustainability. Head chef Kim Tae-hyeong, who used to work for a Michelin restaurant in New York, presents course meals made with seasonal ingredients and plant-based meat. Its main ingredients of vegetables are delivered directly every morning from an organic farm in Paju.

Address	서울시 송파구 올림픽로 300, 롯데월드몰 6층 6F, Lotte World Mall, 300, Olympic-ro, Songpa-gu, Seoul
Tel	02-3213-4626
Menu	런치 코스 Lunch Course ₩55,000 디너 코스 Dinner Course ₩77,000
Hours	11:00-15:00, 17:00-22:00
	forestkitchen.official

포포브레드 베이커리 Bakery
for four Bread

사람, 동물, 지구, 내일을 위한 곳이라는 의미를 이름에 담았다. 천연 발효종, 쌀가루, 유기농 밀가루 등 순수 식물성 재료를 사용해 완전 비건까지 섭취 가능한 빵을 만든다. 종이나 생분해 수지로 포장하는데 궁극적으로 무포장을 지향하고 있다.

Its name means a bakery for humans, animals, the earth, and the future. It serves completely vegan bread made using plant-based ingredients including sourdough starter, rice flour, and organic wheat flour. It packages bread in paper or biodegradable resin, with the ultimate goal of package-free sales.

Address	서울시 마포구 동교로18길 13, 1층 1F, 13, Donggyo-ro 18-gil, Mapo-gu, Seoul
Tel	02-332-2044
Menu	무화과 쌀깜빠뉴 Fig & Rice Campagne ₩7,200 포식이 Posigi ₩6,000
Hours	11:00-18:00 일·월요일 휴무 Closed on Sundays & Mondays
	forfourbread

푸드더즈매터 양식 Western
FOOD DOES MATTER

톡톡 튀는 아이디어로 맛은 물론 모양까지 채소 요리에 재치를 불어넣는다. 파스타 면 대신 주키니를 사용한 베지 라자냐, 순살 치킨 같은 비주얼의 프라이드 컬리플라워가 등이 대표적이다. 당일 수급한 재료로 만드는 신선한 주스, 콤부차 리스트도 다양하다.

The restaurant presents flavorful and witty vegetable dishes with its brilliant ideas. Its signature dishes are Veggie Lasagna, made with zucchini instead of pasta, and Fried Cauliflower, which looks like fried boneless chicken. It also offers a variety of kombucha and juice options made with fresh ingredients.

Address	서울시 서초구 서래로1길 10, 1층 1F, 10, Seorae-ro 1-gil, Seocho-gu, Seoul
Tel	02-593-3322
Menu	베지 라자냐 Veggie Lasagna ₩15,000 프라이드 컬리플라워 Fried Cauliflower ₩15,000
Hours	11:00-15:30, 17:00-21:00 월요일 휴무 Closed on Mondays
	food_does_matter

채식 맛집 50선 | 50 Plant-based

플랜튜드 양식 Western
PLANTUDE

풀무원에서 오픈한 국내 비건 인증 1호 레스토랑이다. 두부로 친숙한 브랜드 특성을 살려 두부카츠 채소 덮밥, 두부 페이퍼 라자냐 등 접근성 좋은 단품 메뉴를 선보인다. 메뉴별 주요 식재료와 영양 성분, 칼로리도 상세하게 제공해 선택에 도움을 준다.

Korea's first certified vegan restaurant, opened by "Pulmuone." The restaurant offers accessible à la carte dishes made with bean curd, emphasizing the characteristic of the brand, such as Rice with Bean Curd Cutlet & Vegetables and Bean Curd Paper Lasagna. It provides detailed information including main ingredients, nutrition facts, and calories to help the customers choose their menus.

Address	서울시 강남구 영동대로 513, 스타필드 지하 1층 I-111호 I-111, B1, Starfield, 513, Yeongdong-daero, Gangnam-gu, Seoul
Tel	02-551-3933
Menu	두부카츠 채소 덮밥 Rice with Bean Curd Cutlet & Vegetables ₩12,900 두부 페이퍼 라자냐 Bean Curd Paper Lasagna ₩15,500
Hours	11:00–21:00
W	www.pulmuonefnc.com

플랜트 다이닝 카페 Dining Café
PLANT

이름처럼 푸릇푸릇한 식물로 꾸며진 싱그러운 분위기의 비건 다이닝 카페다.
병아리콩으로 만든 후무스와 단호박을 곁들인 샐러드가 대표 메뉴로 각광받고 있다.
버거나 파스타 등 친숙한 식사 메뉴와 함께 비건 맥주, 와인이 구비되어 있다.

A vegan restaurant and café decorated with plants just like its name. The restaurant is popular for its signature dish, a salad served with sweet pumpkin and hummus made with chick peas. It serves vegan beer and wine as well as familiar dishes such as burgers and pasta.

Address	서울시 용산구 보광로 117, 2층 2F, 117, Bogwang-ro, Yongsan-gu, Seoul
Tel	02-749-1981
Menu	후무스 단호박 샐러드 Hummus Sweet Pumpkin Salad ₩14,500 렌틸 베지볼 Lentil Veggie Bowl ₩13,000
Hours	11:00-22:00
	plantcafeseoul

채식 맛집 50선 | 50 Plant-based

핀치 브런치바 브런치 바 Brunch Bar
pinch brunch bar

덴마크, 샌프란시스코에서 쌓은 경험을 바탕으로 류제호 셰프가 채소 중심의 요리를 선보인다. 태국식 커리 페이스트에 계절별로 감이나 복숭아를 넣어 만든 시즈널 커리는 산미로 입맛을 돋우는 대표 메뉴다. 친환경 못난이 농산물을 적극적으로 사용하고 있다.

Chef Ryu Je-ho presents vegetable-centric dishes based on his experience in Denmark and San Francisco. Its signature dish is Seasonal Curry made with Thai curry paste and seasonal fruits such as persimmon and peach to stimulate your appetite. It makes a point of using eco-friendly agricultural products including deformed produce.

Address 서울시 강남구 압구정로4길 19
19, Apgujeong-ro 4-gil, Gangnam-gu, Seoul
Tel 010-6711-0522
Menu 시즈널 커리 Seasonal Curry ₩18,000
피스타치오 페스토 파스타 Pistachio Pesto Pasta ₩17,000
Hours 11:30-15:00, 18:00-22:00
일요일 Sunday 11:00-17:00
월요일 휴무 Closed on Mondays

pinch_brunch_bar

해밀 베이커리 카페 Bakery Café
Haemil

햄치즈 마요빵, 카레빵, 브라우니 등 언뜻 보면 일반 빵집과 다를 것 없는 메뉴지만 모두 식물성으로 만든다. 비건인 사람들도 일상의 달콤함을 누릴 수 있도록 우유, 달걀, 버터, 방부제를 쓰지 않고 유기농 밀가루를 사용해 만든다.

The bakery café's menus such as ham cheese mayo bread, curry bread, and brownies seem to not be so different from other bakeries, but they are all made from plant-based ingredients. It makes bread using organic wheat flour without milk, eggs, butter, or preservatives so that vegans can enjoy sweet things like anyone else.

Address	서울시 마포구 동교로19길 101, 1층 1F, 101, Donggyo-ro 19-gil, Mapo-gu, Seoul
Tel	070-7655-0723
Menu	부추만두빵 Chive Mandu Bread ₩3,500 비건카레빵 Vegan Curry Bread ₩3,500
Hours	월-금요일 Monday-Friday 09:00-20:00 토·일요일 Saturday & Sunday 09:00-19:00
Ⓦ	www.haemilbakery.com

흠마켓 푸드 리퍼브 마켓 Food Refurb Market
hmm market

일명 못난이 채소로 불리는 흠 있는 농산물을 다양성의 측면에서 바라보는 곳. 낱개 단위로 구매할 수 있어 특히 1인 가구에게 유용하다. 집에서 만들어볼 만한 추천 레시피와 그에 맞는 꾸러미 채소가 준비되어 있고, 간단한 채소 요리도 판매한다.

It sees potential in deformed agricultural products, also known as ugly vegetables. You can purchase vegetables individually, which is especially good for single-person households. It provides home cooking recipes and vegetable packages for the recipes, and sells simple vegetable dishes.

Address	서울시 용산구 신흥로5길 8 8, Sinheung-ro 5-gil, Yongsan-gu, Seoul
Tel	0507-1373-9716
Menu	채소볶음밥 Fried Rice with Vegetables ₩9,000 고추 접시 Chili Pepper Plate ₩11,000
Hours	10:00-22:00 월요일 휴무 Closed on Mondays
📷	hmm.market

CATCH TABLE

파인다이닝, 오마카세, 핫플 등 4,000개의 레스토랑을 전화 없이 간편하게 앱으로 예약!

레스토랑 예약부터 검색까지 한 번에 손 쉽게!
지금 캐치테이블과 함께 즐거운 미식 생활을 시작해보세요

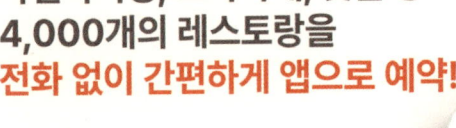

미식의 즐거움을 아는 당신에겐 200만 유저가 선택한 실시간 레스토랑 예약 APP, 캐치테이블이 필요해요

Are you trying to make a restaurant reservation in Korea?
Catch Table is real-time restaurant reservation app service chosen by over 2 million users

---

TASTE OF SEOUL 2022 레스토랑

정식당, 모수 서울 등
Taste of Seoul 2022 레스토랑도
캐치테이블 앱에서
편하게 검색하고 예약할 수 있어요!

전화 없이 24시간 실시간 예약

미식을 즐기는 누구나
날짜, 시간, 인원만 입력하면
원하는 조건으로
쉽고 편하게 레스토랑을
예약할 수 있어요.

한 눈에 확인하는 레스토랑의 모든 정보

레스토랑의 베스트 메뉴,
가격, 발렛, 콜키지 정보에
유저들의 솔직 리얼 리뷰까지!
다양한 정보를
한 눈에 확인할 수 있어요.

TASTE OF SEOUL 2022 Restaurant

4000+ Restaurants including
Taste of Seoul 2022 selected,
such as Restaurant Jungsik,
Mosu can also be easily
searched and booked
on the CATCH TABLE!

Reserve real-time 24 hours without phone calls

Anyone who enjoys
gourmet food can enter
the date, time,
and number of people.
You can easily and
comfortably reserve
a restaurant under
the conditions you want.

All-in-one restaurant information at a glance

You can check various
information at a glance,
including the best menu,
price, valet, and
corkage information
of the restaurant
you searched.

INDEX

테이스트오브서울 100선
100 Taste of Seoul ——— 199

채식 맛집 50선
50 Plant-based ——— 204

*음식 이미지는 실제와 다를 수 있습니다.
*The food in the picture may look different from the actual food.

*영업시간은 코로나19 상황에 따라 달라질 수 있습니다.
*Business hours may vary depending on the COVID-19 social distancing regulations.

한식 Korean

가온	Gaon	강남구	GANGNAM-GU	Map No. 01
권숙수	Kwonsooksoo	강남구	GANGNAM-GU	Map No. 02
꽃, 밥에 피다	A Flower Blossom on the Rice	종로구	JONGNO-GU	Map No. 03
남도제철맛집	Nam Do Jecheol	영등포구	YEONGDEUNGPO-GU	Map No. 04
라연	La Yeon	중구	JUNG-GU	Map No. 05
레스토랑 주은	Restaurant Jueun	종로구	JONGNO-GU	Map No. 06
마포옥	Mapo-ok	마포구	MAPO-GU	Map No. 07
무궁화	Mugunghwa	중구	JUNG-GU	Map No. 08
밍글스	Mingles	강남구	GANGNAM-GU	Map No. 09
봉피양 방이점	Bon Pi Yang	송파구	SONGPA-GU	Map No. 10
비채나	Bicena	송파구	SONGPA-GU	Map No. 11
세븐스도어	7th Door	강남구	GANGNAM-GU	Map No. 12
소설 한남	SOSEOUL hannam	용산구	YONGSAN-GU	Map No. 13
스와니예	SOIGNÉ	서초구	SEOCHO-GU	Map No. 14
안씨 막걸리	Mr. Ahn's Craft Makgeolli	용산구	YONGSAN-GU	Map No. 15
온지음 레스토랑	ONJIUM	종로구	JONGNO-GU	Map No. 16
용수산 비원	Yong Su San	종로구	JONGNO-GU	Map No. 17
우래옥	Woo Lae Oak	중구	JUNG-GU	Map No. 18
윤서울	YUN SEOUL	마포구	MAPO-GU	Map No. 19
을밀대	Eul Mil Dae	마포구	MAPO-GU	Map No. 20
이타닉 가든	Eatanic Garden	강남구	GANGNAM-GU	Map No. 21
정식당	JUNGSIKDANG	강남구	GANGNAM-GU	Map No. 22
주옥	Joo Ok	중구	JUNG-GU	Map No. 23

아시안 Asian

계향각	Gaehanggak	종로구	JONGNO-GU	Map No. 24
도림	TOH LIM	중구	JUNG-GU	Map No. 25
따뚱	DA DONG	서초구	SEOCHO-GU	Map No. 26
미토우	Mitou	강남구	GANGNAM-GU	Map No. 27
무다스벨리	Buddha's Belly	용산구	YONGSAN-GU	Map No. 28
스시메르	SUSHI MER	종로구	JONGNO-GU	Map No. 29
진진	JinJin	마포구	MAPO-GU	Map No. 30
코지마	KOJIMA	강남구	GANGNAM-GU	Map No. 31
팔레드 신	Palais de Chine	중구	JUNG-GU	Map No. 32
플레이버 타운	FLAVOUR TOWN	성동구	SEONGDONG-GU	Map No. 33

양식 Western

한글명	영문명	구	GU	Map No.
강민철 레스토랑	KANG MINCHUL Restaurant	강남구	GANGNAM-GU	Map No. 34
구찌 오스테리아 서울	GUCCI OSTERIA SEOUL	용산구	YONGSAN-GU	Map No. 35
기가스	GIGAS	강남구	GANGNAM-GU	Map No. 36
더 그린테이블	The Green Table	강남구	GANGNAM-GU	Map No. 37
디템포레	De tempore	용산구	YONGSAN-GU	Map No. 38
라망 시크레	L'Amant Secret	중구	JUNG-GU	Map No. 39
레스토랑 알렌	Restaurant ALLEN	강남구	GANGNAM-GU	Map No. 40
레스토랑 오와이	RESTAURANT O Y	강남구	GANGNAM-GU	Map No. 41
레스토랑 온	RESTAURANT ON	강남구	GANGNAM-GU	Map No. 42
메종조	Maison Jo	서초구	SEOCHO-GU	Map No. 43
모수 서울	MOSU	용산구	YONGSAN-GU	Map No. 44
무오키	MUOKI	강남구	GANGNAM-GU	Map No. 45
바위파스타바 한남	Bawipastabar	용산구	YONGSAN-GU	Map No. 46
보르고 한남	BORGO HANNAM	용산구	YONGSAN-GU	Map No. 47
보트르 메종	Votre Maison	강남구	GANGNAM-GU	Map No. 48
비스트로 드 욘트빌	BISTROT de YOUNTVILLE	강남구	GANGNAM-GU	Map No. 49
빈호	VINHO	강남구	GANGNAM-GU	Map No. 50
셰로랑 (구. 르비스트로 남산)	Chez Laurent	용산구	YONGSAN-GU	Map No. 51
알라 프리마	alla prima	강남구	GANGNAM-GU	Map No. 52
에빗	EVETT	강남구	GANGNAM-GU	Map No. 53
윌로뜨	Hulotte	강남구	GANGNAM-GU	Map No. 54
임프레션	L'impression	강남구	GANGNAM-GU	Map No. 55
제로컴플렉스	ZERO COMPLEX	중구	JUNG-GU	Map No. 56
캄포	Campo	강동구	GANGDONG-GU	Map No. 57
페리지	PERIGEE	강남구	GANGNAM-GU	Map No. 58
폴스다이너	Paul's Diner	용산구	YONGSAN-GU	Map No. 59

그릴 Grill

한글명	영문명	구	GU	Map No.
금돼지식당	Gold Pig Restaurant	중구	JUNG-GU	Map No. 60
남영돈	Namyeongdon	용산구	YONGSAN-GU	Map No. 61
벽제갈비 더 청담	Byeokje Galbi the Cheongdam	강남구	GANGNAM-GU	Map No. 62
본앤브레드	BORN & BRED	성동구	SEONGDONG-GU	Map No. 63
삼원가든	Samwon Garden	강남구	GANGNAM-GU	Map No. 64
세스타	Cesta	용산구	YONGSAN-GU	Map No. 65
유용욱바베큐연구소	Yooyongwook BBQ Lab	용산구	YONGSAN-GU	Map No. 66
한우다이닝 울릉	ULLEUNG	서초구	SEOCHO-GU	Map No. 67

채식 Plant-based

로컬릿	local EAT	성동구	SEONGDONG-GU	Map No. 68
마지	Maji	종로구	JONGNO-GU	Map No. 69
발우공양	Balwoo Gongyang	종로구	JONGNO-GU	Map No. 70
베이스 이즈 나이스	base is nice	마포구	MAPO-GU	Map No. 71
베제투스	Vegetus	용산구	YONGSAN-GU	Map No. 72
산촌	Sanchon	종로구	JONGNO-GU	Map No. 73
큔	Qyun	종로구	JONGNO-GU	Map No. 74
포리스트키친	Forest Kitchen	송파구	SONGPA-GU	Map No. 75
플랜트	PLANT	용산구	YONGSAN-GU	Map No. 76

카페 & 디저트 Café & Dessert

강정이넘치는집	Gangjeong house	강남구	GANGNAM-GU	Map No. 77
김씨부인	Kimssibooin	서초구	SEOCHO-GU	Map No. 78
담장옆에 국화꽃 인사동점	CCOT (Insa-dong Branch)	종로구	JONGNO-GU	Map No. 79
메종엠오	Maison M.O	서초구	SEOCHO-GU	Map No. 80
삐아프	Piaf	강남구	GANGNAM-GU	Map No. 81
소나	SONA	강남구	GANGNAM-GU	Map No. 82
아뜰리에폰드	Atelier POND	용산구	YONGSAN-GU	Map No. 83
재인	JAEIN	용산구	YONGSAN-GU	Map No. 84
제이엘디저트바	JL DESSERT BAR	용산구	YONGSAN-GU	Map No. 85
프릳츠 도화점	FRITZ COFFEE	마포구	MAPO-GU	Map No. 86
합 원서점	HAAP	종로구	JONGNO-GU	Map No. 87

바 & 펍 Bar & Pub

까사델비노 청담점	Casa del Vino	강남구	GANGNAM-GU	Map No. 88
르챔버	Le Chamber	강남구	GANGNAM-GU	Map No. 89
뮤땅	MUTIN	용산구	YONGSAN-GU	Map No. 90
바 뽐	Bar Pomme	종로구	JONGNO-GU	Map No. 91
바 참	BAR CIIAM	종로구	JONGNO-GU	Map No. 92
바 피크닉	Bar piknic	중구	JUNG-GU	Map No. 93
백곰막걸리	Whitebear Makgeolli Bar	강남구	GANGNAM-GU	Map No. 94
뱅글	Vingle	성동구	SEONGDONG-GU	Map No. 95
서울집시	Seoulgypsy	종로구	JONGNO-GU	Map No. 96
오네뜨 장	Honnêtes Gens	강남구	GANGNAM-GU	Map No. 97
제스트	ZEST	강남구	GANGNAM-GU	Map No. 98
찰스 H.	CHARLES H.	종로구	JONGNO-GU	Map No. 99
파인앤코	Pine & Co	강남구	GANGNAM-GU	Map No. 100

채식 맛집 50선 50 Plant-based

한글명	영문명	구	District	Map No.
공간 녹음	Nokum Space	강서구	GANGSEO-GU	Map No. 01
남미 플랜트랩	Nammi Plant Lab	서초구	SEOCHO-GU	Map No. 02
더브레드블루	THE BREAD BLUE	마포구	MAPO-GU	Map No. 03
도반	Doban	서초구	SEOCHO-GU	Map No. 04
두두리두팡	DUDURIDUPANG	마포구	MAPO-GU	Map No. 05
드렁큰 비건	Drunken Vegan	마포구	MAPO-GU	Map No. 06
레이지 파머스	LAZY FARMERS	용산구	YONGSAN-GU	Map No. 07
로컬릿	local EAT	성동구	SEONGDONG-GU	Map No. 08
마지	Maji	종로구	JONGNO-GU	Map No. 09
마치래빗 샐러드	March rabbit Salad	강남구	GANGNAM-GU	Map No. 10
마하나 비건 테이블	MAHINA VEGAN TABLE	강남구	GANGNAM-GU	Map No. 11
몽크스델리	MONK's DELI	용산구	YONGSAN-GU	Map No. 12
몽크스부처	MONK's BUTCHER	용산구	YONGSAN-GU	Map No. 13
문쥬스	MOON JUICE	서초구	SEOCHO-GU	Map No. 14
미건테이블	Migun Table	광진구	GWANGJIN-GU	Map No. 15
바이두부	by TOFU	용산구	YONGSAN-GU	Map No. 16
발우공양	Balwoo Gongyang	종로구	JONGNO-GU	Map No. 17
밥풀꽃	Babpullkkot	은평구	EUNPYEONG-GU	Map No. 18
베이스 이즈 나이스	base is nice	마포구	MAPO-GU	Map No. 19
베제투스	Vegetus	용산구	YONGSAN-GU	Map No. 20
비건마마	Vegan Mama	관악구	GWANAK-GU	Map No. 21
비건 앤 비욘드	Vegan & Beyond	서대문구	SEODAEMUN-GU	Map No. 22
비푸스	VFUS	서초구	SEOCHO-GU	Map No. 23
산촌	Sanchon	종로구	JONGNO-GU	Map No. 24
소이로움	SOIROUM	종로구	JONGNO-GU	Map No. 25
스타일비건	STYLE VEGAN	강남구	GANGNAM-GU	Map No. 26
슬런치 팩토리	Slunch Factory	마포구	MAPO-GU	Map No. 27
식물성 도산	SikMulSung Dosan	강남구	GANGNAM-GU	Map No. 28
앞으로의 빵집	appbbang	종로구	JONGNO-GU	Map No. 29
양츨 서울	Yangchul Seoul	강남구	GANGNAM-GU	Map No. 30
오뇽	oignon	강남구	GANGNAM-GU	Map No. 31
오세계향	Osegyehyang	종로구	JONGNO-GU	Map No. 32
우부래도	ooh Breado	동작구	DONGJAK-GU	Map No. 33
움 이터리&베이커리	UUUM EATERY & BAKERY	강남구	GANGNAM-GU	Map No. 34
채근담 역삼점	Chegeundaam Yeoksam	강남구	GANGNAM-GU	Map No. 35
천년식향	Millennial Dining	서초구	SEOCHO-GU	Map No. 36
칙피스	chick peace	강남구	GANGNAM-GU	Map No. 37
카멜스 키친	CAMEL'S KITCHEN	마포구	MAPO-GU	Map No. 38

카무플라주	Camouflage	용산구	YONGSAN-GU	Map No. 39
쿠소이	KUSoy	성동구	SEONGDONG-GU	Map No. 40
퀸	Qyun	종로구	JONGNO-GU	Map No. 41
평상시	Pyeongsangshi	강동구	GANGDONG-GU	Map No. 42
포리스트키친	Forest Kitchen	송파구	SONGPA-GU	Map No. 43
포포브레드	for four Bread	마포구	MAPO-GU	Map No. 44
푸드더즈매터	FOOD DOES MATTER	서초구	SEOCHO-GU	Map No. 45
플랜튜드	PLANTUDE	강남구	GANGNAM-GU	Map No. 46
플랜트	PLANT	용산구	YONGSAN-GU	Map No. 47
핀치 브런치바	pinch brunch bar	강남구	GANGNAM-GU	Map No. 48
해밀	Haemil	마포구	MAPO-GU	Map No. 49
흠마켓	hmm market	용산구	YONGSAN-GU	Map No. 50

100 TASTE OF SEOUL 2022
서울미식 안내서

초판인쇄 2022년 9월 16일
초판발행 2022년 9월 23일
발행처 월간 바앤다이닝(Bar&Dining)
기획 서울특별시 관광산업과
제작 및 판매처 워크컴퍼니
주소 서울시 강남구 강남대로132길 25, 4·5층
Tel. 02-534-5054 Fax. 02-534-5089
가격 뒤표지에 있습니다.

1st Printing Edition Sept. 16th, 2022
1st Publication Sept. 23rd, 2022
Published by Bar&Dining
Projected by SEOUL METROPOLITAN GOVERNMENT (Tourism Industry Dept.)
Produced & Distributed by Walk Company
Adress 4 & 5F, 25, Gangnam-daero 132-gil, Gangnam-gu, Seoul, Republic of Korea, 06044
Tel. 02-534-5054 Fax. 02-534-5089
Price written on the back cover.
Copyright © 2022 by Bar&Dining. All rights reserved.
ISBN 979-11-88155-01-9

이 책의 내용은 서울특별시의 '2022 테이스트오브서울' 사업의 일환으로 제작되었습니다.
이 책은 저작권법에 따라 보호받는 저작물이므로 발행처의 서면 동의 없이 책의 내용을
무단 사용할 경우 법적인 제재를 받을 수 있습니다.

The contents of this publication were produced as part of the "Taste of Seoul 2022" project led by Seoul Metropolitan Government. No part of this publication may be reproduced, distributed, or transmitted in any form or by any means, including photocopying, recording, or other electronic or mechanical methods, without the prior written permission of the publisher, except for the use of brief quotation in a book review.

본 책은 폐지 함유율 20%인 친환경 재생종이 그린라이트로 만들었습니다.